Pages From a World War II Chaplain's Diary

by Clarence E. Walstad

For my mother,

Ruth Marilyn Walstad Kranz,

And in memory of her brothers

who also served in uniform,

Kenneth and Robert Walstad

Peggy Taylor Monahan

Contents

Foreward

by Peggy Taylor Monahan

The author is my maternal grandfather. These letters to his family were personally typewritten by him and privately reprinted in one volume for a limited release upon his return home from WWII's European Theater.

His "dear Sunshine Daughter" is my dear Sunshine Mother, the lone survivor of 3 children. It has been a labor of love to publish her father's experiences for a wider audience, and to put it in her hands during her lifetime.

I have decided to retain my grandfather's original spelling, capitalization, punctuation, sentence fragments and grammatical errors without annotating "(*sic*)" after each instance. I have personally checked and rechecked each word against the document he printed. Nothing has been changed except the formatting of the entry titles, dates and subheadings. Comments in parentheses are his, and mine are indicated by brackets. I hope you will agree this decision adds to the snapshot-in-time charm of his letters. All letters were addressed to his wife Ruth unless otherwise indicated.

Certain terms and phrases are likely to cause some consternation in this day and age of political correctness. I did not soften or omit them to make my grandfather conform to current sensitivities. I can only ask the reader to remember the times and extend grace.

Acknowledgements

Thank you, Lance Tennyson, for being the first outside my biological family to read the original volume in its entirety, and to proclaim: "You MUST publish this for wider readership!"

Thank you, my beloved husband Jim, for photocopying the original privately-printed volume and scanning it into a Word document for editing, which made this book possible. I would have never figured that out!

Thank you, Shannon Page, for picking up the original volume on a slow day at work, sitting on a sofa by my desk, cherry-picking letters here and there for an hour and a half, laughing occasionally, offering admiring exclamations, and directing me to publish this book.

Thank you, Latorial Faison, college professor and poet *extraordinaire*, for walking me through all the publishing options based on your expertise, and encouraging me that the endeavor was worthwhile.

Thank you, Debbie Jaeger, my friend and sister in Christ, for doing the lion's share of formatting the document for publication and assisting in editing the proof copy. You personified "the body of Christ" to me through this process.

Peggy Taylor Monahan

Praise for "Pages"

This diary reads more like a novel than individual letters. Through them, I got to know not only the man but his experiences and hardships that he and his company endured. Capt. Walstad was truly a "man of GOD" whose whole heart was dedicated not only to helping the men he served with in very practical ways, but more importantly, giving them the "truth of the gospel." He wanted them to know, even when some were in their last hours, the saving knowledge of Jesus Christ. Not only did he help in identifying and burying the dead from battles, but he went foxhole to foxhole giving words of encouragement, even while under fire. It was evident that the men in all the units he served had a great deal of respect for him due to his dedication towards them and not just for preaching "at them." Even though his work separated him from the wife and family he truly loved and also the church he had been serving as pastor, he knew this was exactly where God wanted him to be. He was awarded a medal for his sacrificial service to his company and men. This is one book I will enjoy reading again.

Lance Tennyson
Friend

Introduction

[On] August [22], 1942, I was commissioned as a Chaplain in the Army of the United States, with the rank of First Lieutenant. This appointment required several months of correspondence, the good offices of the National Lutheran Council (of which we were not members), the hearty endorsement of both our Lutheran Brethren Synodical headquarters as well as our local congregation in Brooklyn, New York, where I was then serving as pastor; and finally we were required to have two personal interviews with the Chief of Chaplains in Washington, D.C.

During these early days of the war, large numbers of applications were being received for the Chaplains Corps so the officials could afford to be quite selective. In addition, the Church of the Lutheran Brethren had never held a Chaplain's Commission. We did not meet with the academic or theological requirements which had been established nationally by the military. Neither did we have the accepted accreditation of recognized church organizations.

But all hurdles were finally overcome and I was on my way to report to the Chaplains School at Harvard University. I am, perhaps, one of a rather small number who graduated from that ivy league establishment in just six weeks. With my orders in my brief-case, I was shipped off on a troop train to Memphis, Tennessee, where I waited in a Chaplains Pool for a week before I again took a train to my first assignment with the Tank Destroyers who were in training in Jacksonville, Florida.

It was here I had my first experience with the military "snafu" which was to become a part of my life for the next four years. My train arrived in Florida just eight hours after my unit had departed for training at Camp Hood (now Fort Hood), Texas.

I did catch up to them and served this unit through the first army winter. It was not exactly like George Washington at Valley Forge, but neither did we have Hilton Hotel accommodations in our tent city. From Camp Hood I was transferred to Camp Crowder for my last state-side assignment, this time with the Signal Corps.

At the time I received my commission, we were given clearly to understand that chaplains with a family would be kept for state-side duty only. I never saw this in writing so it will probably have to be included in the many delightful rumors which never were based on facts but which did serve to lift our spirits.

In any case, no apologies were made or explanations offered for the orders which reached me saying I was to report to a Field Hospital unit which just then was being readied for overseas duty at Staten Island, New York.

During these ten months of duty in the United States, I had tried with very limited success, to have my family near me. The two boys, Kenneth and Robert, were at private schools. Wife Ruth and Marilyn lived in furnished rooms near the army base at several locations but I was seldom able to be with them. On one occasion they drove all the way from the East Coast to meet me in St. Louis.

I had been given an eight-day leave of absence to be the evening speaker at our Mission Meetings in Grand Forks. Before leaving camp I was able to rent a four-room bungalow and we looked forward to spending some weeks together in our own home again. When I returned from my leave, a message awaited me that we were leaving the states the next day.

You will note that I have passed over almost a year of army life with little reference to my activities. Our journal will have its real beginning as we leave New York Harbor behind and enter upon almost three years of duty in North Africa, England and Europe.

Before beginning our narrative, perhaps two points need to be clarified:

1. Some reader will wonder why I ever sought to become a chaplain. I was at that time serving in a fruitful and challenging ministry in our Brooklyn church. My work was chiefly among the youth. Week by week, I saw dozens, and then scores, of our young men leave for the various branches of the service. Eventually, more than one hundred of them were in uniform. The question burned in my soul: "If I am to minister to the spiritual needs of our youth, should I not follow them?" After much prayer and discussion with the family, we agreed that this was the will of God for the days ahead.

2. I must also offer a word concerning the style in which these pages are printed. It will become immediately apparent that no claim can be made for literary finesse. It will also be noted that much of the material is rather intimate and personal in content. These pages were written as personal correspondence by a heart that was often lonely for our dear family. And they addressed one who anxiously awaited news of a loved one and who prayed day and night for his safe return.

In preparing this unpretentious document for printing, I have not tried to edit out many personal references. I do not anticipate any extensive readership for what I have written. Rather, I have had in mind to share from a father's heart, with my family and closest friends, something of a legacy of these war years in which a father and both of his sons served in uniform, while a mother and beloved daughter clung to the promises of God until Dad returned from Europe, Kenneth from the Philippines, and Robert from the Aleutian Islands.

I was granted my honorable discharge from the United States Army dated January 20th, 1946 as

Captain Clarence E. Walstad, 0 488 466 Chaplains Corps
Division Artillery 2nd Armored Division
European Theater

September 6, 1942 - Parting Festival

Fifty-Ninth Street Church,
Brooklyn, New York. Rev. C. J. Brun, presiding.
(In attendance were Pastors S.E.Bergstad,
Lars Stalsbroten, T.B.Tergesen,
Free Church Pastor Rev. Nelson, and
Navy Commander Bennet Olson)

I think I ought to first of all assure you that I'm not asked to preach any sermon this afternoon. I did that this morning. Therefore, I want to bring a brief greeting at this time. In the first place, let me assure you that we are very happy that it was possible for us to be able to be with you again before I leave for my assignment, and it is my desire that the nature of this service should not be one of expressing our sympathy and broken hearts and shedding of tears. I know and you know that when ties that have been knitted together so closely down through the years are broken, it causes pain. However, that is not what I'm going to talk about this afternoon.

I should like to say that in spite of the pain that must follow such a meeting as this, I was glad for the opportunity to come home today with my family and say good-bye. We are very happy that the friends were willing thus to arrange for this service; so very thankful to my brethren in the ministry who have taken time off to be with us here today and bring us their greetings; to our friends who have blessed us through their prayers, with their testimonies and song.

I think perhaps a word today might be in place in connection with what Brother Tergesen said in regard to the laborers in the Lord's Vineyard. As I saw one place after another in our English work getting empty and our men being called into the Service, and knowing too that our country, in spite of its materialism, had seen fit to appropriate certain funds to make room for the ministry of the Word of God in our Armed Forces, a tremendous challenge came to me. "How can I well excuse myself from at least offering my life for that work?" As we talked it over in our family circle, we agreed that we would take the initial steps, asking God all along the way that if this thing was not in His Plan and Purpose that He should put obstacles in the way so that I would not be able to go through with it. And any man who has applied for a commission in the Service, knows that there are many obstacles in the way. Almost miraculously, it seemed to us at times, the way was opened and a way was prepared until orders came to report for duty on the twenty-second of August. There was, of course, a tremendous crisis that faced us when the hour actually arrived, but again we were satisfied that the Lord had hitherto been opening the way and we would follow on. I have now finished the course prescribed for Chaplains and their training at Harvard University and that has been an eventful experience for me. I have enjoyed it in many respects.

I feel that the fellowship I enjoyed at the school was pleasant. I came to respect our Senior Chaplains, many of them rating as high as Colonels and having spent many, many years, some of them as many as forty, in the Armed Forces of our Country, are now in training schools and headquarters training us younger men. I could not help but feel the sincerity of these men who were to bring the Word of God and the message of Salvation to our men in the Service.

We had interesting fellowships in our dormitory. I brought my wife and my little girl along thinking that I could enjoy my home life there, but Uncle Sam said "no." All of us had to room in the dormitory. Our room was filled. It was made up of one Roman Catholic, one Methodist, one Deep Water Baptist, and one Lutheran, and I felt that since I was the first to occupy that room it was my privilege as well as my responsibility to share the blessings that God had given me in that room. I asked my roommates if they wished to join me in my devotions and I was very happy to hear the Roman Catholic say they would like me to lead them. So the four of us together bowed our knees before our God and we prayed, and it was our privilege to continue our fellowship in the reading of the Word of God until we parted yesterday afternoon.

I'm not going to tell you more about the Army. I am on my way now to my assignment fifteen hundred miles away or more, and the word that we have so far is that we'll remain there a few days and be sent on a few more hundred or thousand miles.

Just what is in store for me I do not know, and on my return some will probably say, "If you knew what it was going to involve, what it would mean to leave your family and your church, would you have gone?" Of course we talked that over, too. I would like to say that every day, at least twice each day, since I left for the Army, I have been asking God definitely to lead me just to that field where he thinks I can work best to His Glory. It is the only thing that I care about. It is the only thing my family cares about. And down in your heart it is the only thing you care about. It is the only thing that matters. And now it does not make any difference to me whether it is over here at Ft. Hamilton or whether it is in the wilds of Patagonia that I am to go. I am satisfied that the door which opens is the door through which God would have me enter and with that I rest content.

I'd like to share with you now just one verse of scripture which has been on my mind. It is found in Philippians 1:21 -- you know it well. "For to me to live is Christ, and to die is gain." Life has suddenly become tremendously precious and dear to millions of people. We do not come to appreciate life until we suspect that possibly it is going to be taken from us, and whereas we as mortals realize that we must some day die, we cannot help but shudder when we know that hundreds of thousands of men will never come back from this present conflict. We're not fooling ourselves about that.. we know it is true. It is not surprising that many of our men become afraid. It is no shame to admit you're afraid. I expect that in the coming months I shall have many men coming into my barracks telling me they are afraid to die. I am not going to tell them that they are poor soldiers because of it. The fear of death is perfectly human and natural. What we need is the reassuring confidence that God is with us in spite of our human fears; and as you reminded us, Brother Stalsbroten, being daily renewed by Him, our human fears will not destroy us and we'll go through with Him in a cause that is right and just; and I agree with Brother Nelson that this world is too small for God and Hitler to rule. If God is going to have any room in this world, the Allies must win in this conflict, but I'm not saying that we deserve to win. God knows that in this world Christianity cannot continue in a totalitarian state. Either the Allies must win or we can be certain that the great tribulation, with the reign of anti-Christ, is upon us. In either event, my job and yours as Christians goes on.

As I leave you today, I want to remind you again that I haven't resigned as pastor of this church. I'm only taking a leave of absence. When you in your homes and at your services pray for your pastors, you may not be thinking of it, but Walstad is included too -- you can't leave him out. As busy as we are in the Army, with our many duties every day, I want you to know that we, too, have time for our daily devotions. And I want you to know that every day, whether on land or sea, in the homeland or abroad, I'll be praying for the church I have loved, and so we'll meet at the Throne of Grace and God will work with you as he works with me. He will work to the Glory of His Name, and we have the assurance that whether we live or whether we die, we are the Lord's. What does it matter whether He lives with us here or we live with Him There? Until we finish the course which He has set before us, there is nothing to be alarmed about, nothing to be worried about. I can honestly say today before God and before you that I haven't the least bit of anxiety at all. It would be most unreasonable if I had because God has given me the confidence that I'm in the place where He wants me to be.

God bless you and keep you.

Part I: 1943

April 14, 1943 - On Our Way: On the North Atlantic

Dear Ruth,

Well, the great day has arrived. I've just returned from the officers' dining room on E deck. We were served on linen table-cloths with sterling silver and beautiful dishes, and by uniformed stewards. The meal consisted of tomato juice, bacon, two eggs, fried potatoes, toast, butter and delicious coffee.

I have spent one night on board. With eight other officers of our unit, I occupy stateroom 121. We have steel bunks with a thin mattress and army blankets. There are two clothes closets, tub bath, latrine and wash-basin. When they turn on the heat it will be quite comfortable. In the meantime we even eat with our overcoats on.

I came on board yesterday with eleven other officers of our unit and about 40 officers from other units to receive instructions to assist in placing the troops when they arrive.

Our ship is a grand one, the S.S.Mariposa. It is quite new, fast and very large. We are most fortunate to have such commodious accommodations. Under normal conditions, we would have in prospect a wonderful trip. As it is, we are never quite unmindful of the fact that this is not a vacation trip.

The morale of the men is good. Wonderful facilities are provided to keep them occupied. They have access at all times to shelves of books, magazines, parlor games, several pianos, victrolas, etc.

But ultimately, morale must depend, not upon outer escape mechanisms, but upon the "soul that is fixed on God" by faith. To be constant and adequate, there must be an assured confidence that God is my Father who cares for His own. The soul that contemplates this glorious truth, sees how nonsensical and absurd fear or anxiety are. "If God so clothe the grass of the field -- will He not much more care for you, Oh ye of little faith?" "Are ye not of more value than many sparrows?" "Therefore take no care." My heart answers, "Very well, Lord, I leave again today the uncharted future in Thy hands. Since Thou dost care for me, my anxiety certainly will not be of help to Thee and will only cause me misery and spoil me for my task of being a help to my men."

Frankly, my heart is at perfect peace. I've been singing,

> "I trust in God wherever I may be,
> Upon the land or on the rolling sea;
> For this I know, He'll guard my soul,
> My Heavenly Father watches over me."

And as I trust the hazards of my way to Him, so also do I trust your responsibilities to Him.

Daily as I set an hour aside for prayer for the safety of our ship and the encouragement of the men, we'll be remembering you, that you may experience that "as thy day so shall thy strength be."

April 17, 1943

This letter will, in all probability, not be mailed for a week or two and perhaps will not reach you for more than a month. But I still have a two-fold reason for writing: I have no one with whom I'd rather be sharing my thoughts than you; and, I like to jot down my impressions and reactions while they are fresh in my memory.

I have today spent my first day on an ocean liner at sea. With bated breath we watched familiar landmarks slip out of sight and then found that only water and sky met our view. There were some exceptions. At least a dozen sea gulls have followed just at the stern of the ship most of the day. They glide majestically in our wake with only an occasional movement of their wings. Their effortless flight must be made possible by using the vacuum or air currents behind the ship. I do not know. But I have watched them with interest by the hour.

Several ships, all of them freighters or tankers, have been met. Some travel alone, others in convoy. Several have signalled us and identified themselves.

We have seen quite a number of both army and navy patrol planes, alert on their routine flights. Several of them were beautifully camouflaged.

During much of the day I have been on deck talking to officers and men. The wind has been bitterly cold and the sun did not show at all until late afternoon. The sea has been beautifully calm throughout most of the day but by late afternoon swells began to roll the ship and whitecaps appeared as far as eye could see.

Have you wondered as I often have what it feels like to be hundreds of miles from land with an expanse of water all about you? To me it seems strange that I experience no sense of loneliness, strangeness or insecurity. All of these emotions I expected. Instead, I feel as though I had been going to sea all my life. I know, as a fact, of course, that one well-placed torpedo could in a moment plunge this entire cargo of persons and material into a cold and watery grave. I am aware of this possibility at any moment and all boat regulations and drills emphasize the fact. But I still have no feeling of insecurity.

I have as yet had no sign of seasickness. The boat has been rolling quite some for several hours but it is actually a rather pleasant lullaby. In addition to the roll of the ship there is also the throbbing vibration from the motors which is especially noticeable when you lie down.

How do we keep busy? Some details that I know would be of interest, I cannot divulge, of course. But in addition to officers' meetings once or twice a day and various types of drills, I'm afraid I spend most of my time walking and talking. The air is invigorating and the cold wind bracing. In spite of crowded conditions some space is reserved for promenading. I have today had lengthy talks with two of my captains which I feel confident will pay dividends in opportunities for spiritual service.

Then I had quite a talk with a rather elderly senior nurse. She was introduced to me as a fellow-countryman and turned out to be a genuine Swede who speaks the native tongue perfectly. But of much greater importance is the fact that she is a genuine Christian of the Swedish Mission. With tears flowing down her cheeks she expressed her joy at meeting another who really knew what it was to be born again and spoke of how her godly father would rejoice to hear that on the same ship was a Christian Chaplain. She is such a motherly individual and. so obviously qualified for her work (she has been in the army more than two years) that I am sure she will exert a tremendous influence for good over her nurses.

Then I have chinned with several Chaplains and spent a couple of hours helping the Ship's Chaplain get all his equipment lined up. In the morning we had a meeting to plan for Sunday and Holy Week. Palm Sunday, Good Friday and Easter on the Atlantic, that will be something!

We have dinner at 7:30 P.M. so the evenings are quite short. Most officers are reading or playing cards. As we travel in constant blackout and the artificial lighting is certainly not the best, I must cut down on my reading as the eyestrain is too much.

Most of all I miss privacy to meditate and pray. Men are coming and going constantly in our stateroom. Furthermore, we have neither table nor chair. I have asked the Chaplain today if he could not arrange for a place of privacy for this purpose but did not get much encouragement. There is no doubt in my mind or yours that the safety of our journey depends more on the providence of God than expert navigation.

Now I must share a good-night promise with you from the Word which God has given me from the 23rd Psalm: "Yea, though I walk (or sail) through the valley of the shadow of death, I will fear no evil for thou art with me "

> "Jesus Christ is my salvation, He will keep,
> From the power of temptation, He will keep;
> Underneath His shelt'ring arms
> I will fear no fierce alarm,
> And from every loss and harm, He will keep."

I pray for you all out on the broad ocean tonight.

April 25, 1943 - MORROCCO, NORTH AFRICA, 66th Station Hospital

It seems just as unbelievable to me as it must to you that I'm writing you from North Africa. This is the land to which David Livingstone first brought the good news of the Gospel and now I'm privileged to be one of his successors. Truly, "God moves in a mysterious way His wonders to perform."

There is so much that I would like to share with you but censorship forbids. We did have such a glorious trip with simply wonderful opportunities for witnessing. We held at least four services daily, personal conferences with from ten to twenty men each day, and there were more than thirty decisions for Christ. Really, it was a spiritual experience for which I would not take a great deal.

April 26, 1943

As you see, I've gone African. We had a fine crossing of the Atlantic on a grand transport, the "Mariposa." We are located in a beautiful country with profuse vegetation and a very temperate climate.

Easter Sunday here seemed a bit strange, of course, but its hope and comfort are just as real here and now as in our cozy home church. We had two services and a good turnout.

How you would enjoy a sightseeing trip with me here! Talk about interesting people, clothes and vehicles! We seldom see a car except those owned and operated by the military but there is every type of cart, hack, buggy and rickshaw you ever heard of. The horses are small but many of them are beautiful Arabian ponies.

Sorry I cannot write more details but at least you will know that I am well, safe and content in the place to which the Lord has led me

April 27, 1943 - Hospital Interlude

I wonder if the sky is as blue and if the birds are chirping as merrily where you are as here.

And I have plenty of time to enjoy nature's grandeur, too, now. I've had an operation since I wrote you yesterday, so I'm confined to the hospital here for a week. I've been going along with an infected big toe nail for two weeks so Sunday the Docs decided it had to come out. They brought me in and put me through so many preliminary tests you'd think I was at least going to have a kidney and two legs removed. Finally, they gave me a shot of morphine about 1 P.M. and by two they had me on the table. I had expected they would give me a local but evidently they decided a general anesthesia would cost no more so a dose of Pentothal-Sodium did the trick. That stuff is really a wonder. They injected it into my arm and I drifted off into a dreamless sleep to awaken at 5 P.M. with a ravenous appetite.

April 28, 1943

I just can't quite figure out why you do not come to visit me while I'm at the hospital. This is the first time in my life I've ever been a patient in one but it seems to me that that is the traditional thing for wives to do. The days would pass so swiftly and pleasantly with you at my side to talk to. As it is I spend as much time as possible reading: long portions of my Bible, studying French and reading again the "Ancient Mariner."

I hope to be out in about a week. My work is waiting I have met some grand Christians here. How true I John 1:7* is!

*["But if we walk in the light, as he is in the light, we have fellowship one with another, and the blood of Jesus Christ his Son cleanseth us from all sin."]

April 29, 1943

I've just had my breakfast of grape juice, cereal, slice of bread, boiled egg and coffee. Sounds good but not very tasty. I've been spoiled these past nineteen years. You always had the knack of preparing even the simplest meals daintily. I'll give you your job back again any time. Steady employment guaranteed.

Five officers leave my ward today. One returns to active duty. The other four are no longer fit for combat duty and will be transferred to noncombat units or returned to the States.

We had prayer meeting in the Hospital last night; fifteen attended. They let me go, too. I even sang a song with my harp. But no one was given a chance to pray. Strange!

April 30, 1943

Yesterday brought a host of visitors. Almost all of my officers were here to see me. Also the day passed quickly and pleasantly.

In the afternoon they changed the bandage. A tough ordeal. Progress is satisfactory.

In the evening a Sergeant and I visited all the wards of the hospital and sang with my harp. The hospital Chaplain distributed tracts. A blessed evening!

I'm to be released in time for my services on Sunday. I'm thankful. I still have to return here to sleep and for change of dressings.

I do hope you were all together for the Easter weekend. I was thinking of you then.

May 1, 1943 [Letter to children]

My dear Bob and Marilyn:

This letter will be the first you have ever received from your Daddy in Africa. It already seems a long time since I said good-bye to you at Fredricksburg, Virginia. Remember? Well, maybe it won't be so long before we can all be together again. In the meantime we each have a big job to do. Know what it is? We are each going to live the very best life for Jesus we know how.

You'd think it fun to visit here for a day but you would not like to live here. There are lots of children but you couldn't understand a word they say. They speak French, Arabian, and I do not know what else. I saw several camels today.

May 1, 1943 [Letter to wife]

Looking at the rainbow hues of the myriads of flowers and inhaling their rich fragrance I think, "If only Ruth could enjoy this with me." Or by contrast, as I see the beggars, the disease, filth, rags and debris and its stench, which clings to you like a garment, I think, "How abhorrent all this would be to Ruth." As I lay abed this morning, the strains of a missionary hymn came again and again:

> "Where every prospect pleases
> And only man is vile."

How true of this land!

I was allowed yesterday to leave the hospital for a little while so I started two of our men building a pulpit for Sunday.

May 2, 1943

They tell us here that the dry season began April 15th but it has now been raining for three days. Mud and water pools everywhere. The sky is still heavy enough to keep up for another week.

I really had a swell service this morning. Spoke on Colossians 3:1-10. Only 44 turned out in the rain, however. We'll do better as we proceed. Have already started plans for Mother's Day.

We are busy as bees getting our hospital set up. We really have a swell building. I'll have my office there and we will have several hundred patients right away. Then I'll have my hands full.

They are not giving us any shots these days but in this malaria infested country we must take atabrine regularly. It does not seem to bother me.

May 3, 1943

Monday I was allowed to leave the hospital so went downtown with my laundry. Out from a sidewalk restaurant who should come running right into me but Milton Engebretson! What a thrill! Both of us were so glad we almost wept. We spent the afternoon together, he had supper with our officers and hopes to join us in a service on Sunday. We are stationed only 14 miles apart. That is grand as long as it lasts.

May 6, 1943

Now that I am getting settled down to regular scheduling of activities, I am going to try to reserve this hour, 8 to 9 A.M. to write to you and for Bible reading and prayer.

I have been busy planning for Mother's Day. It is going to seem strange without a single Mother in the audience.

My thoughts have been much on the subject of Motherhood. Somehow your own mother seems to me such a beautiful picture of faith, contentment, love and industry. Most of all do I thank God for the mother of my own children. Your influence will always be the richest gift we can give them. God give you special grace in these critical times when you must be both father and mother to them.

We are almost ready to set up our hospital as our supplies have come. I got my assistant yesterday. Not a consecrated Christian as I could wish, but nevertheless a capable, thoughtful, moral young man, whom I trust I will be able to win for Christ.

May 7, 1943 - FIRST LETTER FROM HOME!

The sun shines brighter, the birds sing sweeter, the flowers are ever so fragrant, all because I received my first letter from you yesterday. It took just 20 days to reach me.

I get plenty of exercise these days. They cannot give me a car so I have been issued a new bicycle for chasing around. Nature is really beautiful here now. The sun is warm, but the evenings are cool enough for a jacket. It's grand for sleeping if one only had a bed.

Greet friends that I am feeling fine. I remember your words about the Name of Jesus. He shall always have first place in heart and message.

My special job tomorrow besides getting our chapel ready for Mother's Day, will be to go down to the radio station and prepare for a broadcast on Sunday. It is quite possible that I will have this assignment every Sunday from now on together with another real Christian Baptist Chaplain. If I am not mistaken, the program is also short-waved to the USA. I'll find out and who knows but you will be able to figure out a way to hear it each week. Wouldn't that be something!

I have been busy building shelves for library books for the boys. I have gotten over fifty volumes. Besides, I have a large supply of Testaments, tracts and about fifty Moody Colportage books. Much of this I have tucked away in my field desk coming overseas. It weighed almost a ton.

I have this week prepared at least a tentative schedule of services.

Sunday Bible Class, 9 A.M.; Service, 10 A.M.; Radio 11:15; Hymn-sing and devotions at 7 P.M.; Wednesday Prayer Service, and Community sing on Friday evening. Much of my time must be reserved for bedside visitation and I'll have to spend a good deal of time at my office too, so the patients can reach me there with their hundred and one problems.

I have thought that for my Sunday evening services, I should begin a series of messages on the general theme "Twice Born Men" taking characters out of the Bible, who through a conversion experience have entered upon a new life of oneness with God and service toward men. The subject fascinates me and I still think nothing is so convincing as flesh and blood examples of that "old things have passed away, behold, all things have become new."

The one unusual event in this day's activities was this that I received another letter from you. I wonder how many of them get lost. Well, thank God, some of them get through and each one is like a heavenly balm to my soul.

May 9, 1943 - The Lay of the Land

Mother's Day is drawing to a close and I want to write you a few lines before I hike off to bed. It has really been a busy and pleasant day. The sun has been shining gloriously. We had a splendid attendance at our morning service. By far the most enlisted men we have had since I joined up. The Colonel is giving better cooperation every day. I just couldn't ask for a better set-up. I just had a long talk with him about the importance of the spiritual work among the men and he agreed wholeheartedly.

Our radio program went first rate. We had it timed to the minute. We (this other Chap. and I) will have the broadcast every Sunday from now on. It is a wonderful means of testimony as it reaches out to all the camps around and to many units where they have no Chaplain at all. Remember this work in your prayers.

We came home to a good chicken dinner and I studied until 3:30. Then we all hiked down to watch a big parade. They were celebrating the fall of Biserte and Tunis, and the birthday of Joan of Arc and the 200th Anniversary of some military organization. A more picturesque assembly you have never seen. Arabians, Morroccins, French, English, Americans; all mixed together. Everywhere it was teeming with hilarious people. These folks have known the oppression of the Italian and German yoke. Now patriotism and love of liberty are at fever heat. They certainly praise the Americans.

Tonight we had our first evening service. Only 26 turned out but I was not too discouraged. It is the first time they have tried a Sunday evening service; it will grow. I preached on John 1:37-40, we learned "Every Day with Jesus" and I promised them a new chorus each Sunday evening.

Tomorrow the Colonel has given me a half day off so this other Chaplain and I are taking a canteen of water, getting our bikes and hitting out for the country. I want to see the camel caravans and the farmers at their work. I am sure this will prove interesting.

Now I am going to hike off to bed. The nights are cool so if we only had a mattress on our canvas cot and a pillow for our head, we'd sleep well. Quite a few have been sick from all this atabrine but it does not phase me a bit. Tough Norwegian stock, you know.

May 10, 1943

Another day has been made complete by a letter from you. It certainly seems strange to hear that you are still wondering if I am still in the USA. The letter that came today was mailed April 22 -- 16 days ago. Well, that is not so bad anyway for wartime.

Now I am going for the bike ride. When I get home I'll finish this letter. It is a beautiful day. Won't you come along for the ride?

A Glimpse of Native Life

Now my trip to the country is over. What a time we had! We were gone for 4 hours, walked part of the time and took several grand pictures. We went through native Arab sections of the city, where the filth reeks to high heaven and you don't even dare to swallow because of the vermin which you feel will go down, too. Natives sat in their little shops working with leather, metals and cloth. They all sit on the floor, there are no windows and their tools are most primitive.

On the edge of town we came upon a funeral procession, the corpse being carried on a board platform on the shoulders of six men with a large number of wailing relatives and friends moving along behind (read the story of the widow's son of Nain). In fact, the whole trip seemed to turn back the scroll of history 2000 years and carry us back to Bible times. We met caravans of camels with immense loads on their backs, plodding along the dusty trails and little donkeys with loads twice as big as they were themselves, and with the owner perched on top of that. How they ever carry such burdens is a mystery to me. We took a picture of one donkey colt that couldn't have been more than a week old. You never saw anything so cute. Then we came to a place where about fifty women at a pool were busy pounding out sheep hides to clean them and afterward to cure them. They simply soaked them in the water and then beat them with sticks on the rocks.

As we reached the country proper, it might well have been a section of Montana. The land undulates in gentle slopes and is dotted with herds of cattle. Most of them look as though they were imported from America. Great herds of sheep looked much like the American variety except that they have long tails. There were donkeys, mules, horses, camels and goats, all grazing together. All the larger animals are hobbled so they hop along as though they are crippled. They are really in very good shape. There are no fences so every herd has its herders -- usually young boys or old men. One no sooner stops than these boys and even the men clutter around you to beg [for] "Bon Bon" (candy, chewing gum, cigarettes). They hound the life out of you. If you are walking they are under your feet all the time and on a bike they run alongside. You dare not be rude to them as the natives are quick to take offense. So a thousand times a day you explain, "No Bon Bon, no nothing." Since they never tell the truth themselves, they never believe you either. So they tag along until they are exhausted and you yourself are not much better off.

Crops of grain were standing everywhere. Most of it is being harvested now. Oats, corn, and winter wheat are common. The soil here is very productive and I am told they plant and harvest three grain crops every twelve months. We took a picture of a farmer cutting his oats with a little hand sickle. They put about 20 stalks in a bundle, tie them together with a few more stalks and then when they have a load, gather them all into big fibre baskets, balanced on each side of their donkey's back, perch themselves on top of it all, and then make off for home.

We also stopped at two native wells. At one a donkey pulled a rope attached to a bucket made of a part of a truck tire. At the other the same kind of a bucket was used but it was drawn up by a windlass, with a handle on each end. I took a hand at this and the native family laughed in good spirits. The wells are masoned with a native rock and must have been all of 80 feet deep. The herds from all the surrounding community came there to drink. (Read the story of Rebecca in Genesis.)

The highway is good, as it is a main road between cities. It is surfaced with Macadam and is as wide as our highways. About half of the rather busy traffic was made up of Army trucks. The rest were caravans, donkey carts with all sorts of produce, pedestrians, and chiefly natives on donkeys. Most of them greet us cheerfully enough and we respond in French, of which even I have had to learn a little.

I must not forget to tell you about the busses. They are almost as large as the city busses in Brooklyn. But they accommodate at least twice as many. This, for the simple reason that there are surely as many perched precariously on the roof as there are inside. In addition to the humanity on the roof, there may be 50 dead chickens dangling down the sides, a bicycle or two draped at the corners besides massive bundles of filthy luggage. It all comes chugging down the highway, generating gas by burning charcoal. Some mess! I reckon this is the kind of an outfit on which Lester and Mildred came across the desert from our mission field the last time. This must be all for now.

May 12, 1943

I have really been kept busy the last two days. I have prepared my radio talk and had that censored. Then I have been down for a load of newspapers and magazines for the men. Yesterday Milton came to town again and I spent about an hour in the afternoon with him. The rest of the time he sat in my office writing letters and then we went downtown for my first French restaurant dinner. We had good baked white fish and string beans. No potatoes or butter. Cream cheese for dessert. Well, it wasn't bad, but I'm ready to come home for some of your cooking any day now.

Did I tell you that 59th [Street Church, Brooklyn] gave me their old mimeograph? They had it all put in shape for me. I carried it to Virginia and had it crated. Well, it arrived yesterday and we unpacked it and it is in perfect condition. I have asked the Colonel that I do all the mimeo work for the whole outfit. None of these young fellows know anything about a mimeo and they will have it ruined in a month. It makes extra work for me but I have given my Assistant his first lesson in its operation today and soon he can do all of it. I hope it may go through the war with me and that at its close I can return it to 59th for them to keep as a souvenir.

Tonight our first batch of patients are coming in. I cannot tell you how many or from where but it will certainly give us all more to do and I welcome that. I marvel at the amount of equipment that an organization of this kind needs and how well it is supplied by the Government. Believe me, Uncle Sam takes care of his forces. I can begin to understand why it takes so long to open new fronts with the constant flow of supplies needed to keep the units functioning.

Hospital Visits Bring Results

I have been to a neighboring hospital this afternoon visiting three of our men there. They were so happy to see me and I feel certain that this type of work is going to bring rich spiritual results in the army. In civilian life folks have so many coming and going continually. Here the others are so busy with their own duties that the Chaplain seems to be the only friend they have who can spend some time with them.

May 17, 1943

Today is Monday once again and another week is on its way. It appears that I am to have another busy week and for that I am thankful. No one is as unhappy here as those who must sit and twiddle their thumbs. There is practically nothing to do with leisure time and those who do not like to read find life terribly boring.

I remember, too, that today is Norway's 4th of July. I reckon this is the third year they have commemorated their day of freedom under the cruel yoke of Nazism. But they are a strong, patient people and never have the fires of determination burned more fiercely in their hearts. It will not be easy to get these occupied countries to sit down dispassionately at a peace table and formulate equitable terms. The brutality and carnage of the Axis these long years is making it almost humanly impossible for men to think of much else than vengeance and reprisals. It is just there that we, at each peace table, sow the seeds of the next war. And so the race goes on in its vicious circle. The flower of each generation's manhood is butchered while those who are physically or mentally handicapped are left at home to propagate the race. The natural resources as well as manufactured products, intended by a bountiful God to add to our comfort and enjoyment are prostituted to feed the god of war. Farms, homes, entire cities, are pillaged and deserted, while the people who can escape scatter by the millions like lost spirits, wandering about homeless, starved, learning to steal and pillage. Debts are mounting so hopelessly that the world will be bankrupt. When the nations have wasted themselves utterly until from sheer exhaustion they sue for peace, almost 100,000,000 men who have been trained for years to hate, kill and destroy, come home to find their jobs taken over by others, their thinking completely out of stride with civilians, and the world seemingly having left them behind -- what a problem in adjustment!

Yesterday I had a big day. Bible Class at nine with just five present. Service at 10 where for the first time we had patients present. There were about 30 of them there. 11:15 radio broadcast. I enjoy that work and rejoice to know of the hundreds of American boys at various outposts who have no services, and who in this way hear the gospel. At 3 P.M. I went to two of the wards and conducted services for the men who because of contagious diseases, are not allowed to attend public services.

With all of them I left tracts and copies of Scripture. At 7 P.M. I had my vesper service with a good hymn sing. We learned a new chorus and I preached on "Andrew, Soul-winner." I had at least six Christian folks there and I enjoyed that service the most of all.

May 18, 1943 - A Forty-Mile Bikeride

I took my half day off in the afternoon yesterday and started out on my bike. After riding about five miles I decided to keep going and visit Milton Engebretson. So it got to be a trip of 40 miles before I returned at 7 P.M. It was much too hard a ride over the hills on that heavy bike and I'll not repeat the performance soon.

I've been on the run all day today. We have gotten in so many patients today that the receiving office is still full at 9 P.M. I go to every patient in the hospital each day though I will not be able to do that much longer. Quite a number of them are in very bad shape and I am so glad to have a chance to minister to them both physically and spiritually. A number of them are able to be up and around and for these I have provided reading matter and games. I discovered one of them today is a real artist so I have had him prepare two posters for church services. He does good work and he is tickled to have something to do.

We had our first prayer meeting tonight. There were just four of us there but enough to claim God's promises and experience his nearness. Will keep right on regardless of numbers.

May 20, 1943 - Fresh Eggs for Breakfast

Today will go down in history as a red-letter day. We had fresh fried eggs for breakfast. It's funny how you miss simple things. Dehydrated foods, which make up almost our entire diet, are often quite tasteless, though thoroughly nourishing. What I'd give for a glass of milk or a piece of pie, or perhaps a bit of ice-cream.

I managed to get a radio for the patients today. I was as tickled as they were. Just now a news report tells us of floods in southern U.S.

We're still waiting for mail. I hope we have to take a day off to read it when it arrives. In my spare moments I am reading "The Confessions of St. Augustine." It is a ponderous, theological volume which I should have studied years ago.

May 21, 1943

I'm losing faith in V-Mail. I never get any so maybe you do not get all the letters I have written either. So we'll go back to Air-Mail and see how that works.

What a hectic day this has been. I was in my office at 6:30 this morning and it is now 10 P.M. and I have several jobs yet to do. With all these new patients, our staff of nurses being doubled, our enlisted men finding time hanging on their hands with very few places where they are allowed to go, a lot of work has been dumped in my lap. Ordinarily I would not be required to do this morale work but the officers assigned these jobs are so busy getting the hospital set up that they simply cannot get around to it during the day. So I do a lot of their work during the day and much of my own at night. However, tomorrow I'm getting help. Two Red Cross workers have been assigned to our unit. That will be a tremendous relief and much more can be done for the men than I could possibly do.

My neighbor chaplain has been sick in bed all week. Yesterday they brought in a young chaplain from the field who is really very sick. He's the young man who roomed with me at Harvard and whose wife you met. I'm feeling fine and getting brown as an Indian.

My assistant is working out O.K. He is slow in his work but cooperative, polite and willing. I keep him busy, I tell you. But of course I cannot work him longer than from 8:00 AM to 5:00 PM.

I met a nurse the other day who had heard me preach in Brekke's church in Seattle. She is a Christian and took part in prayer at our service last Wednesday. Most of the nurses seem friendly toward Christianity and appreciate the work one does for the patients but the vast majority make no pretense of godliness. Many of them are a lot older than you would expect for this strenuous life. Several of ours have completely grey hair.

"Be strong and of good courage, be not afraid neither be thou dismayed, for the Lord thy God is with thee whithersoever thou goest" (Joshua 1:9) is the verse God gave me today. What a blessed assurance. I cannot doubt its truth for daily I sense His comforting and guiding presence. And I'm sure there is a blessing there for you, too, so I pass it on as I say good-night.

May 24, 1943

Normally folks catch up on their letter-writing on Sunday, but that is my busiest day. I was in my office at 7 A.M. as usual and just kept going all day until I locked up at 10:30 P.M.

Sunday is an especially long day for patients. That day more than any other they think of home and miss their loved ones. So in addition to my four services, I try to get around to most of them, sit beside them and talk and where patients are not too ill, conduct a little song service. Their appreciation touches your soul.

With so many patients, there is less chance for the doctors and nurses to attend services. They really put in strenuous days. Some of the non-Christians have shown a real interest and go out of their way to explain their absence from the services. As I went through their ward visiting in the afternoon, two of the nurses stopped me to say, "Chaplain, I hope you offered a special prayer for those of us who could not be at the service this morning. We tried so hard to get through with our work so we could get there. We really needed it today."

I met one more Christian soldier yesterday and two Christian nurses. The soldier is stationed here and said he'd be coming every Sunday. The nurses have a unique job which I'm not permitted to explain to you here in this letter. They are Pentecostalists. They have no Chaplain in their vital assignment and wanted Christian literature. I supplied them with a good quantity, we had a prayer service dedicating all of it to the Lord for His use and we sent them on their way -- perhaps never to see them again. What a wonderful thing it is when a nurse or doctor is a sincere Christian. It seems to me that many more of them would want to be, with all their opportunity to see what a difference faith in Christ makes to the sick and dying. But actually very few seem to take Christ seriously. I do feel I have won their confidence and God will give the opportunity to speak the right word to them. Just yesterday after the service a Lieutenant said, "Chaplain, that was a great message this morning and led me to believe that you have the answer to a problem that has been perplexing me for a long time. One day this week I want to talk it over with you."

We have been having exceptionally fine weather. It clouds over at night so one expects rain but the next morning the sun shines again. I suspect the dry season is beginning. That will mean that all the beautiful flowers will soon disappear. However, there is considerable irrigation -- when the water supply allows it. You would have been thrilled by the beautiful bouquet of three dozen carnations and the gorgeous display of one dozen immense white lilies which adorned our chapel Sunday. I stood with one of my Catholic Majors before the service admiring them and said, "Major Kelly, there's a sermon just in looking at those lilies." He replied, "Chaplain, that sermon has already been preached by the greatest preacher." "Consider the lilies of the field, how they grow."

If those ships ever start bringing in our mail, they are going to have a real cargo. Our mail orderly hardly dares to show his face as he comes empty-handed each day from the Post Office.

God gives a wonderful sense of His nearness here. I feel so confident of His care that I haven't a suggestion of anxiety for my safety. It is not always so easy to be at ease about you and the children. I think of the problems and decisions which confront you and your concern about me. But may God teach us to rest completely in the promises for every need.

May 27, 1943 [letter to son]

Dear Kenny,

Well, I have just finished boxing five rounds and playing three games of volley-ball so I think I'll write you a few lines while I cool off and then I'll take my bath and get ready for bed.

Our men have fixed up a good boxing ring and smoothed the ground for a good volley-ball court. I have entered them in both the volley-ball and soft-ball leagues. All the various army units in the vicinity play one another and there is some mighty fine competition. All of us brought with us from the States a good supply of athletic equipment which the army furnishes free. It certainly is a life-saver in this country where the men have nothing to do in the evenings.

You see, with the many different nationalities and political factions which are found here, it is dangerous to go out at night unless you go in a large group. Everything is totally blacked out after 8 P.M. so that most anything could happen -- and it frequently does.

Other than athletics, we have very little physical training. Being a hospital unit, our men do not have a great deal of military tactics beyond the basic training which they had the first few weeks they were in uniform. Since then they have been trained as ward boys, doctors' helpers, litter bearers, clerks. We operate very much like a big hospital in the States and have some mighty fine equipment. Our Government certainly supplies us with nothing but the best.

How is your enlistment in the Navy getting along? They have a big job to do in this war. Some folks talk as though one of the branches of the service is going to take care of the big push into Europe. That's a lot of foolishness. Germany with her Allies is no push-over and it is going to take the complete coordination of land, sea and air forces to break them. You can be sure we will not try it until the whole stage is set. Right now, Hitler has the jitters and we'll keep jabbing away so he does not know when or where to expect the knockout punch. But that won't happen tomorrow.

If you get into it, and I'll not say you shouldn't, it does not make so much difference where you serve. The important thing is that you do the best possible job of soldiering every day. That is the way each of us can help to get this thing over as soon as possible.

May 30, 1943

Today is Memorial Day and Sunday. It has been a great day with a very busy schedule in the morning and then a peaceful afternoon.

I started the morning with going off for a Jewish Chaplain at 6:45. His schedule is so full that he has to have a meeting for our men at 7:30. From 8:30 to 9:00 I was busy getting my chapel in order. We were to have communion today and also special flowers so a good deal of preparation was necessary. Then at 9:00 we had an interesting Bible Study on "Who Gets the highest Loyalty in your Life?" At 10:00 we had a good service. I spoke on Abel; "He being dead yet speaketh." I emphasized that some people so live and die that they continue to speak after their lips are silenced. Whereas some seem to make a big splash for a short time and after they are gone, nothing constructive or lasting was left behind. How come Abel still speaks after he is dead? A few key words in the text in Hebrews 11:3 tell the secret: 1) Faith, 2) Sacrifice, 3) Righteous. As a result, God testifies on his behalf that his life has been worthwhile. That is the final test -- God's approval. Then I made some application to Memorial Day which reminds us of those heroic dead of our own country who did not count their lives too great a price to pay for perpetuating the ideals of liberty, truth and opportunity. They speak to us today from the military burial fields, almost encircling the globe and now many of them from the very desert sands where we are encamped, bidding us carry the torch further.

Have you ever thought how aptly this thought of a memorial lends itself to the message of a communion service? I went on then to speak of how the sacrament about which we were gathered was also a memorial service. These elements are the tokens of One who gave His last full measure of devotion that we might enjoy the liberty of the sons of God. He, too, being dead yet speaketh. Of what does He speak in this sacrament? 1) Of the awful sinfulness of sin. What means this broken

28

body and this shed blood if not the price that was paid for my redemption? It tells me that both my body and soul were under the curse of sin and needed to be atoned for. Christ held nothing back but gave His all that we might have life. 2) It speaks to me of the love I owe One who has thus loved me. Nothing less than my all is a worthy or even reasonable sacrifice to lay at His feet.

It was a blessed hour. A captain told me afterward, "Never have I been faced as at this service with the need of being spiritually prepared by faith and forgiveness to partake of this sacrament."

Immediately after this service I jumped into a truck and left for the radio station. My message today I thoroughly enjoyed giving. I expect we may hear from some of the men out in the field in response to it. I received no criticism from the station on the nature of the message. One Lieutenant gripped my hand and said, "That was fine, Chaplain. I listened to every word of it." It is something when even the announcer will listen with something more than professional interest.

Came home to have pork chops for dinner. We have really been having very good food this past two weeks. Much better, I am sure, than what you civilians get. Our cooks do a better job of preparing it, too, than many army cooks.

After dinner I delivered mail to patients and sat with several of them and talked. Last night I went to all who are in contagion and those confined to beds giving New Testaments to all who would accept them. I gave out about thirty. Today we set up two radios so over one hundred of the patients heard my broadcast. That is really an opportunity for which I thank God. I am putting in an awful lot of time on it but I consider it one of the most worthwhile projects I have.

After the one-day's splurge of mail, it has died out again. So once more we sit waiting. But it's not so bad now knowing that you have heard that I have arrived safely and knowing that you have your plans for a pleasant and profitable summer. God has ordered all things well for us. May His kind providence teach us to trust Him more when the way is dark. It is little credit to us that we grumble when the way is closed and only praise Him when our way is bright. Faith will sing the doxology in the tempest and see the rainbow when the clouds are darkest. What fair-weather Christians we are after all. God help us to grow in trust and confidence.

June 3, 1943

Today at the chief's office I met a Chaplain who had been with me at Harvard and had also been at Memphis, Tennessee. In all his time in the Army he has never been assigned to a unit. He was shipped overseas without an assignment and has now been here for six weeks, knocking about, waiting to be put to work. Talk about a trial.

It appears we have a pianist in our outfit finally. The Red Cross worker is really good. She is obviously more at home playing jazz but has played for her former Chaplain each Sunday. She is a funny combination since she is of true New England vintage, with all of its aloof refinement and yet she bangs away at that keyboard like a maniac.

I have had two fine spiritual talks with the men today. One of them told me that though he comes from a Presbyterian home he has never read the Bible in his life until he accepted a New Testament from me last Sunday. He has now read Matthew and Mark and came to ask questions today. I gave him a booklet on what to look for in the Bible, especially the message of Salvation to his own soul. He is a college graduate. The other chap was an older man who was thoroughly fed up on the Army and disgusted with life. He, too, has begun to read the Bible but I fear his mind has begun to break and he may be discharged from the Army.

I have not gotten a letter from a single soul since I came here except from you and the children. I guess all in the States have forgotten me.

June 4, 1943 [letter to daughter, age 9]

Dear Sunshine Daughter,

Now I have gotten two letters from you so I better get busy and write you one or I suppose you will be mad at me.

I am afraid I cannot send you the ticket to come over here that you asked for. You see, if you lived here you would have to wear dresses that dragged on the ground, you would go bare-footed all the time, you would have to have holes punched in your ears so they could put in ear-rings and then you would have to have all your hair shaved off except one long braid in the middle of your head, which is left there so the Angels can lift you up by the hair to heaven if you should die.

Besides, you couldn't talk either American or Norwegian. You would have to learn to say, "*Bon jour, monsieur, comment allez vous?*" (Good-morning, sir, how are you?) And then I will answer, "*Tres bien, merci, mademoiselle.*" (Very well, thank you, miss.) Now that would be quite a job, wouldn't it?

Then you wanted to have me bring you some coconuts. That I cannot do for I have not seen one since I came here. They have lemon and orange trees, and they grow dates and figs, but you would not care to eat them after these Arabs with their dirty hands, full of sores, have picked and packed them. But I'll send you something for your birthday.

I pray for you every day and I know that you pray for your Daddy, too.

June 5, 1943

It is Saturday night and I am practically ready for my Sunday services so I'll get started on my letter. I'll be preaching on Zechariah 2:4 in the morning. "Run, speak to this young man." This command of God I must heed not only as a minister of the gospel but, under present conditions, also in place of mother, wife and teacher. 1) Why this special concern for the young? Because they are inexperienced. Because they have great temptations. Because youth is essentially honest. Because they are important members of the community. Because their character will soon be fixed. 2) What shall we say to them? They have a soul to save. They have a God to serve. Sin, though attractive, is costly. Their capacities are intended for more than fleshly gratification. There is a judgment day coming. Now may God help me to get this truth across to them all.

This evening we have had quite a program here. A whole group of RAF boys stationed near here put on an affair for the hospital. It was really very good though, of course, here and there it had to border on the smutty and suggestive. They had a wonderful violinist who would be a credit to any concert. He played four numbers. They had an excellent Baritone who sang three pretty ballads. They had a choir of fourteen voices that really harmonized beautifully. In addition, there were a couple of comedy numbers and then an orchestra that dished out insane jazz. But really, as soldier affairs go, it was good.

June 9, 1943

We had one of our inevitable parties last night. The nurses entertained the male Officers. I am just plain glad that I do not need to put in an evening at these things. It is understandable that the world must have its entertainment and to dance and drink is its measure of a good time. As long as it does not interfere with duty there is not too much that can be said against it from their point of view. However, I prefer to be free from the pangs of conscience the morning after, which they must suffer. I am also spared the humbling experience as I face my fellow officers the next day of thinking what an ass I made of myself in the presence of them all.

Of course, I had to put in my appearance there. That is Army and the Colonel makes it plain that he expects it. So far I have not felt it necessary to rebel although I make it a matter of prayer and am willing to do what Christ would have me to do. My task is merely that some time during the evening I enter, pay my respects to the Colonel and whoever is host or hostess and then leave. So last night I spent the evening working in my office until 9:30 on my radio sermon and had a swell time. Then I had to get on my bike, ride to our quarters, get dressed and shaved, and then ride over a mile in the dark to this affair. I was home again and in bed by eleven. This morning the Lt. in the bed next to me asked wearily as we were dressing, "Chaplain, did you have a good time at the party last night?" I answered, "Lt., I do not go to these parties to have a good time. I go in line of duty and it's not a very pleasant duty."

Last night one of the Officers brought a nurse over to where I was standing, talking to two Officers who were not dancing, and said, "Chaplain, Miss D wants the next dance with you." The other Officers added their bit, "Come on, Chaplain. You would not turn a young lady down. Be a sport." They all knew perfectly well by this time what the answer would be and would, no doubt, have been thoroughly surprised had I said, "Yes." But they must have their fun. Finally Miss D had a chance to get in her own request. I answered them all kindly, "It is very generous of you all to be so concerned about my having a good time and I am sure the same generosity will enable you to understand that to me as a Christian, dancing would neither be proper nor enjoyable." A hush fell over the group and abruptly the subject was changed. It is truly remarkable how the Lord is with you in these situations and gives the word that strikes conviction to the heart. May they be given to see that it is not myself that makes the difference, but Christ in me.

A Call to a P[O]W Camp

Our area senior Chaplain telephoned me at noon today to ask, "Chaplain, how wedded are you to that unit of yours?" I replied, "That is quite a question to answer on the spur of the moment and over the telephone." He said, "I'll send a car up for you if you can come down." O.K. Right here I had better go back a bit in the story. Two days ago I had brought to my attention a situation in a unit which to my mind was intolerable. I brought it to the Senior Chaplain asking that if possible he make investigation and seek to rectify matters. He went to work on it and found that one of the most serious difficulties was the Chaplain, who had no drive, no prestige or respect in his unit. He must be moved where he will be under direct supervision of others. So here is the Senior Chaplain calling to ask if I would be willing to take this job. It is a tough assignment, in the desert, with the most primitive accommodations. But those are not factors to be considered. I am better able to put up with such things than perhaps 75 per cent of the Chaplains. That which is worse is that I will have to start building from the bottom. That is very much the same situation as I found here.

The factor that must weigh most is the tremendous challenge of the task. It is a hospital unit in charge of a German and Italian prison camp. I will have under my care about one thousand prisoners and about the same number of our own guards, nurses, officers and enlisted men. The whole bunch need encouragement, the real power of the Gospel, as well as a real friend.

Well, this is the proposition I had to face. I told the Chaplain quite frankly that the physical hardships involved did not in the least disturb me. The difficulty of the assignment only presented a challenge for service. I said I was willing to make any change which in his judgment was for the good of the service. Finally I said I had left every detail of my Army career in the hands of the Lord and if I was needed for this post I would take it as the Lord's leading. He was mighty swell, and spoke many kind words of which I will share some with you, that you may thank God with me that He has enabled me to serve in a manner that has been a blessing. He said that he personally hesitated to make the assignment as he was reluctant to lose my Christian fellowship in this area. Also he knew of the good work I was doing in my present unit. I was the one man available to whom he could turn that place over with the assurance that all would be done that could be done. He wanted me to understand that as disagreeable as was the task, it was at any rate an expression of the confidence of their office in my work. I sincerely thanked him and we went off to the top men of the North African theatre to see if the plan met with their approval. It did. The official orders are expected to come out Monday.

There still remained the matter of breaking the news to my CO. Of course the Chaplain says it will go through whether my Colonel approves or not, but they do want to consult him and if possible get his approval. As it happened the Colonel was not in so the Chaplain spoke to the Adj. and the ex. Off. Both were shocked speechless. They finally said, of course if the orders come down there was nothing they could do about it but they were sure the CO would be indignant. Then they both chimed in (and I thought that was mighty decent of them), "If Chaplain is to be taken from us and given a big job like that, you will at least have to give him his Captaincy." The Chaplain was afraid that could not be because of the new ruling which requires to be a year in grade. Since the new camp is about an hour's drive over good roads from where I am now, the Chaplain has asked that I continue my weekly radio broadcast. I am happy for that.

Now will you agree that this has been a day? I may not sleep very well tonight but I am perfectly at ease about it all. While I have been here I know I have done what I could and can leave with a clear conscience that I have by the grace of God lived the Gospel among them and "Have not shunned to declare unto them the whole counsel of God." Out there would be new and rich opportunities. The hardships are nothing. I have chafed under the comforts we have enjoyed here. It's not right, while men are suffering by the hundreds of thousands for the same cause. No, since there is no immediate opening to be up at the front, I am glad to take this task and trust God to meet every task with me.

June 13, 1943

Well, it has happened as I expected. I have just now returned from my Col. office where I have read the orders of my change of assignment. So it is all settled. I am to get the new Chaplain lined up here tomorrow morning and then in the P.M. will go out to my new place to confer on the work there. I will have to pack everything I have tomorrow evening and move on Tuesday. Thus I am on the road once more. "We have here no continuing city."

My Colonel had quite a session with the senior Chaplain yesterday. He fought the thing to the last ditch and when he saw it was impossible to avoid the change, he went to bat for my promotion and insisted that since I was being put to all the trouble of moving, of working a unit up from the bottom and when my services were so valuable out there that no one else could be found and finally since it was such a big place, that at least I ought to get my Captaincy. Well, no promises were made and I'm not optimistic about it coming through.

You would have been impressed with my good-bye with my Colonel. He shook my hand at least four times to express his thanks for my work. His chin trembled and he also started to cry when I left. He assured me that he is going to put in once again for my Captaincy and

34

besides is enclosing in my permanent military file, a letter of commendation for my work.

I announced my leaving at the services this morning. It's funny how many attachments can be made in just five months when you have gone through dangers and hardships together. Several of them began to weep. Two have since sent notes to my office to say they are not equal to coming in to say good-bye so are doing it this way. The Christian life and the Gospel of Christ makes its impression and will live with these folks.

June 15, 1943

Yesterday the CO drove with me out to my new assignment. It is located smack out in the burning desert without a tree in sight. Everyone is housed in tents, with the wind hurling particles of sand about continually. No more sea breezes. Say, this will be something like what I came over here for. Some real rugged Army life with a job big enough for three.

Out here one sees the real effects of war in all its ghastly reality and I will certainly have many hair-raising experiences. My old CO just boiled that I should be put into a hole like this. I am not feeling at all sorry for myself. The physical hardships are more than compensated for by the challenge of a tremendous task.

June 16, 1943 - "I was in prison and ye visited me"

Did Christ also mean Army prison camps? Undoubtedly He did. That is a good share of my task these days and I do find it interesting. I have now taken over and am trying, in the midst of sandstorms, to get my office tent in order. It is some job and everything you own is gritty with dirt in a few minutes. Your own person is no better. One is simply filthy and water is rationed to one bath a week.

I have really a bigger job than I had first thought. When I reported for duty I found that the hospital was only a small part of the camp proper. Though technically assigned to the hospital, I was soon advised by the camp CO that I was responsible for the entire camp. He immediately assigned me Post Chaplain. Just how many services I am going to have each week I do not know.

Then nothing has been done in athletics for the men. The old excuse that they have not had time to arrange it, stinks. We have time to do anything that we are really interested in doing. They have two immense crates of athletic equipment that the Government issued them before they sailed and these have never even been opened. There is not a book for the men to read, although they are entitled to 200 of them free, if they just take the trouble to go for them. These are just a few of the things that I must take care of right away.

June 25, 1943

This is an interesting place. I am having so many new experiences. In many I see the hand of God working with me. Just an hour ago I visited a ward (I have a couple dozen of them) where there were four victims of a Jeep accident two days ago. One Lt. is still only semi-conscious as he turned over with the Jeep five times. Another Lt. I had quite a talk with. He came back from the front just a week ago. He said he had not told this to others but that that experience had changed him from a reckless God-forgetting youngster, to a seeker after God and a reverence for all things holy. He told of how eight German planes had strafed him and his 12 companions for 15 minutes until almost all of them were dead and he had come out of it without a scratch. He told me he had been on his knees praying aloud as the bullets spattered around him. Then this car accident. As he came to, he did not know if he were dying or what, but he lay on the ground praying that God would save his soul and if possible let him get help for his buddies. He was able to stagger down the road four miles to our hospital. One of the others may not live. I certainly talked seriously with this Lt. and urged upon him that he must not only let the terror of dying drive him to prayer but that he truly seek Christ as his Saviour.

June 28, 1943

Coming home from my radio broadcast yesterday, I stopped where there had been an accident on the road. Two Army trucks, one a great oil truck with trailor and the other a 2½ ton, had crashed head-on. The drivers had been blinded by dust. The large truck was burned to a crisp. A guard told me that all our men had been taken to our hospital. I found that two colored fellows that had been in the cab of the large truck, were bandaged from head to foot. The one, I was told, had no skin left on his body, except on the soles of his feet. The other was almost as bad and was so distorted with swelling you could hardly tell that it was a human being. Neither of them could talk, neither am I sure they could hear; there seemed little hope that they live long. I asked the nurse if she could let me have just a minute with each of them and then knelt in prayer. The whole ward of men remained silent until the prayer was
36

ended and we had committed the soul to God. How I wonder if they had ever heard the gospel so that even in their pain and semi-consciousness, the Holy Spirit could bring back to them the message their souls needed. The one boy died at 6 p.m. and will be buried today. His wife and little boy are being notified. The other man will probably die before the day is over. The third lad in the truck was hitch-hiking. He was not burned, as he was thrown by the impact so his collar-bone was broken. I reminded him that it was not just luck that he had been spared, and asked him if he had thanked God for his deliverance. That he hadn't, but he was glad to have me express his gratitude in prayer. He gripped my hand as I reminded him that this was God's warning to turn to Christ and that he owed God the rest of his life.

Last night we had a memorial service in the colored boy's outfit. It was really touching to see the love these men had for one of their buddies. Their white Officers were there and one spoke a few words and then broke down and wept. They had something of a Negro Choir. After I had spoken on "How God makes no mistakes in those He calls away" they sang, "So we'll have a little talk with Jesus, and we'll tell Him all about our trials; He will hear our faintest cry, and He'll answer by and by."

I simply could not hold back the tears as these simple-hearted folks sang, and as I walked down the road to my camp in the bright star light, I too "had a little talk with Jesus" about you and the kiddies and was comforted again in the knowledge that you are safe in His care.

June 30, 1943

Most of my work so far this week has been business. With the tremendous population we have, actually a large city which has sprung up over-night, there are bound to be many administrative problems for the Chaplain as well as for the other departments. For instance, each prisoner is paid so much per day. Part of what he gets will go to pay for toilet articles, tobacco, etc. So it is part of my job to see that each of these hundreds of men fill out the form authorizing us to make the deduction (10¢ per day) and then see that he gets the supplies that he has paid for.

July 3, 1943

Tomorrow is our Independence Day. We are to celebrate, according to General Eisenhower, by doing double the work we ordinarily do. And why not? There can be no doubt that the most worthy commemoration of our freedom is this that we rededicate ourselves to more earnest efforts, that freedom's torch shall burn with even brighter flame, until its glow shelters all those oppressed nations, who today bleed and weep. May God hasten the day.

Last night I had the grandest meal since coming to Africa. An engineering officer took two others and myself to a beautiful hotel overlooking the sea at Fedala, Morocco. The dining-room had a very high ceiling, each table its bouquet, genuine silver and white tablecloth. Beautiful soft drapes adorned the massive windows, and just outside, the surf rolled lazily up on the sandy beach. The first course was ice-water. If I had had nothing else I would have been quite content. But no, we had leg of lamb, beets, string-beans, bread and jelly, fried potatoes and then watermelon for dessert. It is months since I have enjoyed a meal like that. Afterwards we had a few minutes in the garden that surrounded the place.

Last night I had an interesting experience. I was in my office until late and after completing my sermon preparation, I got my harp and began to sing. My office is located right in the midst of the hospital tents, the walls of which are rolled up. Men were stretching their necks out on all sides of me to hear. Before long a group gathered at the tent door. So I sang of Christ and mother and home. Many of these P[O]W's can understand a little English.

All could follow the music. Afterward I asked them if they would sing some. Several had been members of church choirs in Germany in better days and since so many of our Lutheran hymns are translations from the German, we were on familiar ground. We harmonized on "Fairest Lord Jesus", "Oh, Sacred Head now Wounded", "When I Survey", and then ended up by singing "Silent Night" in five languages. Several of them broke down as the familiar strains floated out on the night air. Afterward I spoke to them a little to say that though we are enemies there are some things we all have in common: home, mother, God and the love of Jesus, who came to earth that Christmas Eve. Poor lads, they too believe in the cause for which they have been suffering in this malaria infested hole, for almost two years.

Our enlisted men have been working almost day and night carrying out four times the amount of work for which this hospital was organized. Added to this all these patients were dumped into their lap almost overnight so they had no time to prepare their own quarters, because, of course, the sick and wounded had to come first. Until last February our men have been sitting out in the sun and dirt to eat. Now we have gotten a shelter over their heads and burlap for wall so they have some semblance of cleanliness even though they still have only a dirt floor. It is really wonderful that the health of the men is so good under these conditions, but fresh air and physical activity seem to keep up their resistance. In spite of primitive conditions the Army does exercise the strictest vigilance against all possible infections. We wash our dishes in three changes of boiling water after each meal and once before we eat. Our cots are all caged in with Mosquito Bar and at night we must smear on insect repellent. Four times weekly we take atabrine. Any man failing to take it is subject to Court Martial. I have been vaccinated for smallpox three times already. You cannot get through our gate to our area without showing the certificate of vaccination. But in these primitive and crowded conditions common sense tells you that every precaution must be religiously adhered to. So we are doing all we can to come home to you healthy and strong.

July 15, 1943

You would hardly believe me if I told you that as I write, a forty-piece German band is tooting away just fifty feet from my tent. These men were all captured with their instruments and now are permitted to come over to the hospital area to entertain the patients. It is better than fair music, too. Our men may listen only if they stand in a group apart from the others and do not express their appreciation of the performance. One of the most difficult things for our men to remember is that a few days ago these same men were blowing our buddies and brothers to bits and that they are still our enemies plotting escape and revenge. The traditional American attitude of sympathy and even admiration for the underdog wants to manifest itself in friendliness toward these men. It just cannot be done. We find it necessary to keep reminding them to keep their distance.

Well, I must tell you about my new assistant. He is a Christian though he himself will not say so. He is from the Free Methodist group. I had a long talk with him the first day I was here as I outlined my program and policy of work. Of course, I asked him about his relation to God. After having heard of what the other Chaplain had told me of him as a consecrated Christian, I was flabbergasted to hear him say that he could not call himself a Christian. He went on to say that he was trusting the Lord as his Saviour but had never attained to that position in grace where he could say he was a Christian. Then he told me that a Christian in the true sense of the word was one in whom all possibility to sin was eradicated and whose complete compliance with the will and plan of God was without a slip. Well, he is too honest to ever say he has gotten that far. Unless he succeeds in later years in making a hypocrite of himself, he never will attain such perfection. Would to God that I could show him that believing in Christ, we are complete in Him. That though in humility and honesty of soul we must continue to our dying day to pray, "Forgive us our sins," yet in the sight of God, through Jesus' Blood, we are as though sin had never stained our souls. Praise God that salvation is a miracle of grace, not a striving reformation.

He is a good boy and very conscientious. He puts in long days and believe me, there is plenty to do. He has been trying to get this office tent of mine in shape since I came. We have no floor in it yet and as the wind blows the dust and sand every day, we must dust and dust and yet you grab dirt every time you pick up something. I am going to try tomorrow to put some cloth coverings over some of my books and papers.

I have today been to town to get some supplies. I got a supply of toilet articles for patients and also quite a quantity of books for my men. Then I received the promise of a grass rug and some wicker furniture for our nurses' day room. They have a tent for this purpose and believe me, it is pretty bare. The carpenters expect to get a floor in there by next week so it may add some little touch of comfort to their otherwise drab existence. They really are putting up with more than it seems right to ask of women. Most Army officers that I have spoken to about it agree that this is positively no place for a woman and would send them back to regular hospitals if they had their way. But evidently the War Department considers male nurses unable to do the job. Most of them are older women. Several are married.

You've never been in jail, have you? It's really quite an experience spending all your days under the eyes of tramping, armed guards, with high barbed wire fences all around you and required a dozen times a day to show your pass in order to move about. Actually, the prisoners are well treated, almost too well perhaps. The sick and wounded are given exactly the same care as our own men. They sleep on steel beds with mattresses and sheets. Most of them really appreciate what we do while, of course, some grumble continually. The Germans even in prison clothes and under the point of a tommy-gun are arrogant, hold their heads high and salute with the snap and manliness that is hard to keep from admiring. Many are veterans of more than two years fighting in this fever-ridden and heat-blasted country and yet they are perfect specimens of health. Most of them are very polite and we have no trouble with them. I obtained permission today to let them use athletic equipment and they play with fine enthusiasm. At night I can hear their voices ring as they sing over in their area. They usually sing as they march. What a tragedy that such robustness, enthusiasm and vigor must in one generation after the other be turned into channels of destruction.

The Italians are entirely different. Their faces are usually a blank. There is a spirit of defeat, subjugation and listlessness that is difficult not to despise. The difference is no doubt partly due to the fact that they have lost all enthusiasm for this war and feel that their "friend" Adolf, has left them holding the bag and doing his dirty work. Even more, it is due to their national temperament. There is no question, I think, that they are a sensitive, emotional people with delicate tastes that run toward the Arts rather than the sciences, toward poetry and waltzes instead of physical stamina or violence. They are not soldiers and I doubt if they ever would be even with a worthy cause to fight for.

We use almost 100 of the prisoners to work in the hospital as ward boys, orderlies, etc., among their own men. Many have served in medical units in their own army and are well qualified. They take orders and like their work. But one amusing angle was told me the other day when one of these arrogant Germans came to the ward officers and asked if he could not be given another assignment. They were surprised, for he was one of their best men and they inquired what was the matter. He drew himself up to his full height and declared, he had never taken orders from a woman and could not bear the ignominy of having a nurse tell him what to do. Well, he is still suffering this terrible humiliation.

July 19, 1943

Another Sunday has gone and a blessed day it was. In the morning I enjoyed much liberty in speaking on Matt. 7:13-14. Afterward I drove to town for a wonderful broadcast from the Red Cross. About 300 men were present. We had a soldier's octette and a quartette to sing for us. God gave needed grace to preach the message which I have sent you. I also received a letter through the Radio office from a major up at the front requesting a copy of a sermon I gave recently that he might read it to his men.

After the broadcast, I together with a Captain and two Sergeants were invited for dinner to the home of a Miss Grant. She is a missionary to the Arabs in this area. She has been here for seven years. She is under the North African Mission and a product of the group at Keswick, New Jersey. I did enjoy that contact and hope later to see her at work among her people.

I returned to camp to make my afternoon visits and then the evening service. Sunday is a glorious day and God is so very precious in His Word.

July 20, 1943 [letter to daughter, age 10]

To Marilyn,

Dad has just finished playing his first ball game in Africa. Our officers played the officers from another outfit. We beat them, too --12 to 11. I got three hits out of four times at bat. Pretty good for an old man, isn't it? We are supposed to play again tomorrow night against another outfit but it is prayer meeting night, so I'll not play.

I still think you would not like to live here. The native children do not go to school and never learn to read or write. They never go to church, either. They seem to have no games to play and just spend their time sitting around in the dirt. Last Sunday I was in the home of a Missionary who invited these little children into her mission and teaches them Gospel songs, to sew, and tells them stories from the Bible about Jesus, The Children's Friend. He loves them even though they are so dirty and ragged. I wonder if they ever have enough to eat and they always beg from us when we go down the street. We must thank Jesus that we were born in a Christian country and then do all we can to let others know about Him too. I wonder if Jesus wants you to be a Missionary when you get big? Do you still think so? It is the biggest job in all the world.

July 22, 1943

Last night I had an unpleasant mission. The Red Cross worker stopped in to deliver to me a Radio-gram for one of my boys, informing him that his father had died a month ago. I called the boy in and tried to break the news as gently as I could. He was a Catholic. His mother had died a number of years ago so he now feels rather lost. I was so glad to have a chance to tell him what a friend and confidant Jesus could and would be to him if only he would accept Him. I left him with a word of prayer which he repeated after me word for word until his voice became so choked with tears that he could say no more. I am now sending a Radio-gram for him, to his family.

We had to get rid of one of our German medical officers yesterday. He is a typical Nazi, arrogant as a peacock. We made the mistake of treating him as a man and a gentleman with the result that he has gradually gotten to the place where he thought he could dictate how the hospital was to be run. The final straw was when he had one of his men beat up by about ten others because he had said that when he got to America he was going to try to become a citizen. Well, there are ways of putting a man of that calibre in his place and it has all been ironed out now.

July 23, 1943

This place has taken on quite a picturesque appearance the last few days. A whole group of Native French Morrocan troops under the leadership of flashy French officers have taken over. Most of them I suppose have done nothing but fight and drill for ten years and they certainly are a snappy outfit. We enjoy watching them, but it is going to be mighty hard on the prisoners. After the Germans and Italians have ravaged their women, stolen their cattle, ruined their homes and plundered all in their paths, it is rather too much to expect them to be gentle with their captives. Now that the tables have turned, they will have their pound of flesh, you may be sure. By religion they are all Moslems and as fierce and ruthless as these people have been for generations. Many of them are the barely civilized mountain tribes formerly known as the Berbers from the Atlas Mountains and which have been more or less (mostly less) tamed and united through that great statesman and soldier, General Lyautey. That is the name to remember in this country. This French officer since 1904 subdued one wild tribe after another, finally united them into a semblance of order and began an era of progress. Building contractors, teachers, doctors, sanitation officers followed close behind his conquering legions and all this country honors him even today with monuments, parks and festivals.

July 24, 1943

Sunday was a pleasant day with services in the morning. At the first I really had a blessed hour. I spoke on Paul's statement, "I have fought a good fight, I have finished my course, I have kept the Faith." It really burned in my soul and proved very practical. Let me share an experience which illustrates how wonderfully the Lord leads. In my introduction I told of how a shepherd got sheep through water by taking a lamb in his arms to be followed by the mother and others. You have heard me tell the story from our own farm. So I was making the application of how God often interferes with our cherished plans in order to draw us to follow himself, even to the taking away of our little ones. Afterward a soldier came up to take my hand. He could not speak at first but after clearing his throat several times and wiping away the tears, he said, "Chaplain, this is the first service I have been to in a long time and I am so glad I came. You see, just before I left the States, our only child, ten months old, died. I became so bitter with life and especially with God that I have turned away from the Bible entirely. Today I have seen for the first time that God was kind in taking our baby. Kind to our baby and kind to us. I am so glad you spoke as you did. I am going to trust Him again." Well, here's the interesting part: That illustration has not gone through my mind for a year or more, I am sure, and when I went into the pulpit that morning I had no intention of using it. It just came to me. God knew that man would be there and would need that word.

Today we have had quite an experience. Just as we were going to breakfast a rifle shot rang out. We went to see what had happened although shooting is getting to be a common occurrence around here. I arrived just in time to see an Italian prisoner writhing in death with a bullet through his heart. He had, presumably, been trying to escape and had in one fleet second been plunged into eternity. Of course, thousands are dying every day just as violently and suddenly. They too, like this man, have a wife and small children who love and wait for Dad's return just as our dear ones do. I followed the case all forenoon, was present at the autopsy, called in the Italian Catholic Chaplain for the last rites and by noon had no appetite and a soul full of sick loathing for this devilish business of wholesale and ruthless killing and hate. Some may praise the marksmanship of the Moroccan who dropped a man at more than a hundred yards with a bullet plumb through the heart. Personally, I could only revolt at such wanton waste of life and the rebellion of man which makes wars necessary. Rebellion against a God who two thousand years ago offered them a Prince of Peace that they might live in peace and safety. "Oh Lord, how long, how long."

July 29, 1943

I haven't written anything to you on the war for a long time. Really, I am sure you are much better posted than I. I do not get to hear a radio more than twice a week. The paper "Stars and Stripes" brings us rather prompt reports but the coverage is brief and usually deals more with spectacular and unusual happenings than the deep underlying strategy and policy of the whole picture. That is understandable. Everything here moves so fast and everyone has so many jobs to do that the necessary thought and time for clear evaluations and insight is simply out of the question. That is left to the swivel chair strategists on Park Avenue. We are too busy getting the dirty work done and providing food, shelter, equipment and medicines.

However, it has been thrilling to know that our big push toward the continent is progressing even ahead of schedule. Our troops had the soft part of the attack on Sicily. We faced the Italians who have been ready to quit for a long time and will now with the resignation of Mussy, undoubtedly seek collaboration and peace terms. The British and Canadians over on the other side, facing the German installations had a much heavier time of it. Hitler will have a hard time now keeping Italy in line. Many German officers here even concede that we will win the war but it will take two years.

August 1, 1943 - An Arab Meal

I'll have to tell you this time about the dinner I had last night. It was a real Arab place and though I was not sure I would get anything I could eat, I would not want to leave this country without having eaten one real native meal.

So I took off with eight other officers in a truck. We drove about twenty miles and came to a whitewashed, high wall. We drove through the archway with chickens scattering every way. A goat scampered away and a beautiful horse was tied right by the door of the house.

The Native lady met us; she could speak French and one of our Captains, who speaks that lingo well, was our spokesman for the evening. She welcomed us through a low arch into a flowered courtyard with tiled bird baths and cool benches everywhere. As this place was a sort of restaurant, there were several little dining rooms around the edges of this court. We were led to one of them. Before we entered we were invited to take off our shoes (we had been warned about this so we were all careful to have on socks without holes). Our room had a thick homespun rug on the floor. There were mattresses all around the room covered with lovely cretone material. Large pillows were everywhere. We sat down on the mattresses and crossed our legs under us and then were ready to start the meal.

First they brought in glasses of hot tea. It was flavored with strong mint but was fairly good. Afterwards a young man brought in an immense copper bowl and tea kettle. We held our hands over the bowl while they poured water over them and then gave us towels to wipe them. That done, they brought in the first real course which was a platter about two feet across with five or six roast chickens. We were given no tools to eat with but were expected to dig in with our fingers and take what we wanted. There was a deep oily gravy into which we dipped bread made of sour dough and with a thick crust. We really enjoyed that dish but our hands and mouths were plenty greasy when we had finished.

Then they took away the platter and gave us a chance to wash our hands again. Next they brought in another platter just as big, full of little balls of highly seasoned meat that looked and tasted something like hamburger and which I suppose was made of horse meat. This we had to fish out of deep gravy with our fingers.

When they had taken away the meat balls, they brought in another immense platter piled high with some kind of ground cereal around the edges and in the middle was steaming egg plant and boiled mutton with some beans and raisins. The dish is called "Kush Kush." The cereal had some oil mixed in with it and we were supposed to dig our fingers into it, get out about a thimble-full, roll it in the palm of the hand until it became a ball and then eat it. That dish I did not care much for and only barely tasted it.

Once again they poured water over our hands and we certainly needed a wash. Next they brought in fruit, very tasty slices of melon and green grapes. That was the best part of the meal to me.

Finally they brought in coffee in glasses and some cakes. The coffee was as black as tar and so bitter I barely downed one swallow. The cakes were like small apple turnovers without apples. Not much.

I must tell you what to me was the most interesting part of the meal. I asked the officers if they would object to my asking the Blessing as we began to eat. They said, "Go ahead." The Arab woman was there. She is a Mohammedan. She stood quietly as I prayed and then said, "Perhaps the American's God will bless my home, too. This is the first time a Christian has prayed in my home." I told her I was sure He would because He loved us all.

After the meal, we got up and stretched our cramped legs and then went out to put on our shoes. It had gotten dark by then as it had taken us almost three hours to eat. When one of the Captains got home, he found he had put on the shoes belonging to another officer who belongs to another camp. Say, did we laugh at him. Now he is trying to figure out how to get his own shoes again.

August 4, 1943

We are now reaching the close of an unusually blustery day. In the U.S. you would surely say that it would blow up a rain before morning. But here it only blows up sand. All day it has been coming in like snowdrifts, into my office tent and our sleeping tent. You eat and breathe sand, your hair is stiff with it, and the water in your eyes manages to keep the eyeball clear by depositing it in gobs in each corner. It works its way into your bed so you grind your hide against it all night. Your clothes are saturated with it, of course, and look a mess. All in all, before we can come marching through Times Square, resplendent in brass and braid, we are going to have to undergo a thorough overhauling.

It is surprising to see how folks bear up under it. They grin through the dirt and keep on the job. In fact, it has been our observation that morale is lowest in those organizations which are situated in the big centers and enjoy the most privileges. I suppose the reason is that there they have a chance to see others who get more than they do and so are always discontented. Here no one has anything so there is nothing to covet. Only thoughts of Victory, home, loved ones, a sweetheart, and a growing determination to get all this over with as soon as possible so that life can once more be ours.

August 4, 1943 - Life in a Prison Camp

This last weekend was especially difficult. Many little things just went wrong with various persons failing to keep their promises and letting me down. I am afraid my last two letters haven't been too inspiring. I am out of it now. "He restoreth my soul." How faithful God is!

Yesterday we were told that the censors would now allow us to tell a bit more about our work here. Only location, size and movements are taboo. I do not know just how much I have told you before, but I think you know I am located in one of several prison camps here in North Africa. We take in both Germans and Italians. They are organized into Compounds, and have their own officers who are responsible to our officers for maintaining discipline, getting the men fed and lined up for work each morning. The officers are allowed to live in tents by themselves and, depending upon their rank, are afforded quite a few privileges, even to having an orderly. The officers are not required to work unless they wish.

The enlisted men are called out each morning in groups, to do different jobs. Some are carpenters and there are buildings going up here continually. Many of them dig drainage ditches, clean up the area, haul gravel, to try to settle this everlasting dust. They always work with a U.S. guard, who watches over them with a loaded rifle and of course they are searched every time they go in and out of their compounds. As I have said before, most of them are quite cooperative and our biggest job is not to keep our people from humiliating them, but from admiring them. None but the Chaplains are expected to talk to them except strictly on business. I am free to mingle with them as I wish and have many interesting talks with them. Most of the Germans are still sure that they will win the war and that within two years. Some of us have different ideas about that.

August 7, 1943 - A Trip to Mara Kesh

I had no chance to write last night because I was away on a trip. I had a wonderful time and have seen some of the most beautiful buildings and scenery since coming here.

The Red Cross worker for our district invited me and another Chaplain to ride with him to a town down south about 150 miles. He has an old Army Chevy which nevertheless is more comfortable than an army truck. It was to be a ride inland so we were prepared for a hot trip and believe me, we were not disappointed. The wind was like a furnace blast. The air was hazy with a powerful desert storm.

About every fifteen miles we stopped at some guard posts where a few soldiers would be stationed in a single tent and mighty lonely. We'd leave them some reading and writing material, speak a few words with them about the Lord, and then drive on.

We arrived at our destination in time for a late supper at a hospital which is operated by three of our doctors and five nurses from this outfit. They take turns of a month each to go down there and take charge. The hospital is a French one of which the Army has taken over one of the four floors to care for American fliers. I wish it were possible for me to describe the beauty of the place. It is surrounded, as are almost all buildings in this country, by a high wall. You drive through a large gate and then under immense palms to the entrance where wide plate glass doors receive you into a refreshingly cool vestibule done in tile Mosaic and gray marble. I have not seen more beautiful hospitals in America. The hospital grounds include many acres of fruit trees and vegetables of many kinds. These must all be irrigated, of course, but native Arab workers provide cheap labor. I walked in the gardens this

48

morning before breakfast and it was hard to believe I was on the edge of the Sahara Desert.

Last night after we arrived we took a drive out to the Red Cross Club. I have never seen as swell a one even in America. The building and. grounds were strictly new and modern. I understand it had been left not quite completed by the French. We bought it, finished it up and now have a veritable swanky place for the men of that area.

Today before we left, we were urged to have dinner at a Hotel which we did. The beauty of the wood carvings, the spacious lounges, the breathtaking Mosaics, the artistic indirect lighting simply beggars description. I was so glad to get some post-card pictures of it that are perfect except that they do not show the gorgeous color. Some of our officers stay there. I do not think they know there is a war going on.

We went in to eat from white table-cloths. Can you imagine that? We had a vase of roses on the center of the table. Through immense plate glass windows which swung open, we could look out on the gardens that surrounded the place.

As we sat eating, who should sit down at the next table but Bob Hope and Francis Langford. They are here with their whole troop to entertain the men in Africa.

I had hoped to get down into the native Arab section of the city to purchase something I have been wanting to get for you but which is so high here that it is out of the question. But there have been some cases of Bubonic Plague down there so we were not allowed to enter. We then started on the long hard ride home. But the trip had certainly been worth it and now I must prepare a sermon for tomorrow,

August 9, 1943

We have been having quite a number of deaths here lately. A German died last night after we thought he was over the crisis with diphtheria. Tonight I am almost sure an American boy will die with meningitis. He is unsaved and seems to have little concern for his soul. I went to see him late this afternoon and will go again tonight. The whole outfit got another shot two days ago for diphtheria. On the test I was immune so I escaped. Many of the others got real sick from it. One gets sick and tired of all these shots.

They are really getting in earnest about getting us into condition around here. Added to our calesthenics each morning, they are now giving us road marches of several miles, twice a week. Fortunately, they start us off at 7:00 a.m. The heat the last two days has been terrific.

Today I was simply no good until 4:00 p.m. but this evening I would not mind working until midnight and I probably will.

August 11, 1943

I have just finished my morning's devotions from I Samuel. How wonderfully God led David through dangers, misunderstandings, the machinations of wicked men and all because his all was on the altar of God. I had such a grand day yesterday with four blessed services. I take care of two prison camps now and for the present we have a great number of troops. One of the units was activated at Fort Snelling and I had a grand time talking to the boys last night as most of them come from around Minneapolis. At the camp where none showed up for service a week ago, I had over 100 men at my two services. Some of them had not been to a service or seen a Chaplain in more than a month and many came forward to express their joy at hearing the gospel again. At the morning service the Holy Spirit was so very near. I was myself so gripped I broke down several times. Men wept aloud and several asked for prayer. In the evening when the invitation was given, ten men responded and I dealt with several of them afterward. Three others asked if I could come back this week so they could talk with me. I am planning to spend all day Thursday at that camp and talk with those who come.

In the afternoon an intelligent young man came to me to say, "Chaplain, I need your help. Last night I lost almost $30.00 gambling. The money does not mean so much but I begin to see that I have become a slave to the habit and there isn't much I can do about it." At the service this morning I had spoken on the verse: "And ye shall seek me and ye shall find me when ye search for me with all your heart." This man said, "God really spoke to me. I think now that this is my only hope. I have been thinking through the philosophy of religion for years. Now I need its power in my life." As plainly as I could, I showed him the way of salvation and then we had prayer together. I have good hopes that God will bring him through.

Thus it is that when the work begins to drag and one feels discouragement, God sends the encouragement needed and shows that His Word is accomplishing that whereunto He has sent it. God grant us to sow the seed in faith, even with tears, believing that the harvest will come.

August 13, 1943

Well, today is an anniversary and were you here we would certainly find some good restaurant to go to for a good dinner tonight. It is just a year today since I was commissioned an Officer in the U.S. Army. It has been an eventful year. It has certainly had its share of heart-rending partings, momentous decisions, perplexing situations and weary loneliness. It has also had its share of joys, great spiritual victories and compensations for losses. My soul this day would sum it all up in the words of the prophet: "Great is thy faithfulness." How wonderfully He has kept us all and revealed to us new horizons of spiritual possibilities. Outstanding in my thoughts is the realization of the beautiful courage you have shown.

I had a wonderful day yesterday. I told you that I was to spend the day at the other prison camp. You see, I am responsible for both of them now and that one really has in it more American troops than this. So I went over first thing in the morning. They have a hospital there, too, so I first visited the patients there and then went to the day room where the men congregate to read and write. The Red Cross has put in a few tables and chairs and I arranged to get them papers and magazines as well as parlor games to keep them busy. Here I set up a little office for the day, hung out my Chaplain's flag, and prepared a book table with tracts and Scriptures. I then went about talking to the men and they began visiting the tract table and by mid-afternoon magazines and papers were almost entirely laid aside and everywhere men were reading tracts. Then they began coming over for consultation. There was the usual run of inquiries about looking up relatives that are over here, pay that they had not gotten, and troubles at home. But the joy of the day was the fact that several came to speak about their soul. One told me (he's from Oklahoma) that he had once been a Christian, had drifted entirely away, but had definitely come back to God last Sunday night in our service and that this week had been the happiest for months. Another chap who had a Christian mother, told of how he had rebelled against God until after four months in the Army, he saw he could not do without Him, and had given his heart to Christ alone in his tent.

We had arranged to have a service in the evening at 7:30. I expected five or six there and when they told me that they were paying the men in one of the companies that night, I began to wonder if I would have that many. When 7:30 arrived we had 43 men present. I was thrilled. Well, we sang quite a number of songs that I let them request and then I spoke to them. Four or five sat there with tears streaming down their cheeks, unashamed. One lad sat with his head in his hands and wept out loud. When I gave the invitation, 14 of those lads asked for prayer. I knelt with them on the floor and together we went to the Lord in prayer. The rest of the fellows sat reverently with bowed heads. Praise the Lord!

August 18, 1943

It is just the time of evening for a pleasant walk with you. A cool breeze has come up after a scorching day. The grazing cattle out on the sun-baked fields are busy finding some dried up straw to fill their middle before the night. The roads have begun to be busy with every type of camel caravan, mule cart and donkey pack. They will be on the road all night as it is too hot to haul loads in the daytime. They are on their way to the city markets and if they do not make it tonight, will pull off to the side of the road about ten a.m., get a few strands of straw out of a bag for the animals and then stretch out full length on the ground in the burning sun and the noise and dust of passing vehicles of these crazy Americans who do not have sense enough to take off in the heat; there they'll sleep until the cool of the afternoon and then be on their way once again. It seems not to matter at all when they get home. I have seen broken down wagons at the side of the road for two days or more, while repairs are leisurely made. There are seldom women on these trips but on market days, the whole family evidently turns out. Then early in the morning you hear them hurring to barter; vegetables, grain, cloth, sheep, goats, cattle, donkeys. On the outskirts of almost every city is a big area for their market. Here they set up ragged tents for the day and place their wares on racks or on the ground for display. They do some shouting but mostly the scene is characterized by confusion, dust, the stench of half rotten meat lying out in the sun and black with flies. It takes lithographing post card companies to make the scene picturesque. In reality it is sordid, filthy and depressing.

Last night I had another wonderful service at the other camp. A real spirit of revival is manifest there. Last night fifteen men definitely accepted Christ and afterward I was hardly able to get away because of all who gathered around to talk to me. Last night one of the fellows from Minneapolis told me he is hoping to return home.

One of these days they are going to let me go home, too. I suppose it will not be so very soon although there is certainly reason to hope that the war on the western front is headed for a real climax this winter. That still leaves us the tremendous job in the Pacific. Wonder if all of us will be shipped over there. Whatever the military or political picture, we are sure as Christians that God would let it all end tomorrow if man would only humble himself.

August 22, 1943 - Return to Casablanca

We are now taking care of American boys again. We haven't very many here and we will not stay long. It is intended as a rest period and reward for the big job we did in the last spot. The building is almost as nice as the first I was in and the living quarters are even nicer. I can hardly believe that there is practically no dust.

My service this morning was well attended considering we are not even unpacked yet and quite a number are still at the old station getting that cleared up. It was good to see quite a number of patients present. I sang "God Understands" and spoke on the "Enduring Mercy of God" from Psalm 136.

August 26, 1943

The breeze from the ocean here makes it quite cool at night and it is not until about 9:00 a.m. that Old Sol really gets in his work. However, the heat here cannot compare with our last camp. Besides, we have trees in our yard and birds twitter there most of the day. All in all, God has given us a wonderful rest camp.

Almost all of the patients here are American boys who will never return to duty but will, as soon as they are able to travel, return to the States. They are some of the casualties of war In some ways they are more tragic than those who die. Most of them are shell-shocked neurotics. They are generally depressed and need to be helped and entertained continually. The Red Cross is pretty well supplied with facilities and two women workers are with them continually.

A Polish Pianist in Concert

Did I ever tell you that I went to hear a Polish pianist the other night? He played in a small theatre which was well-filled. I was disgusted to see only a handful of soldiers there and one nurse. They would rather spend their time at a bar, of course. However, that did not detract from the wonder of the performance for those of us who went. I have the folder of the program, written in French which I will certainly keep as a souvenir. I have never enjoyed such an evening in Africa, in an esthetic sense. You know I have heard very few world famous pianists and I had always felt that hearing expert playing over the radio was quite equal to paying a couple of dollars to attend a concert. But what a difference! The very performance, facial expression, gyrations of the body, the intensity or laxity of his muscles, simply make you live in the composition. It was a revelation to me.

I am glad to hear of the books you are sending. They will be more welcome than you think. I am just remembering that you have asked me several times if you could send me anything. Some of the boys have even had food sent to them, but I see no sense in it. Very little of it is fit to eat when it arrives and when you think of all the work and love and tenderness that goes into its preparation, it is a shame to have it so wasted. So I'm just going to live on my dreams of the best cooking in the world, for this guy, until the day I sit with my long legs under our own table and feast on dishes fit for a king.

This is the Army. My big interruption came this morning as the CO asked if I would speak to the men a few minutes together with other officers. I always accept such an opportunity for, while one cannot really preach to them, it does afford a contact. Well, it develops that the special purpose of the meeting is to announce to the unit that their detachment commander has, at eight this morning, received notice that he is to be transferred to another unit 200 miles away and will report for duty there tomorrow. Just like that. Neither he nor any of us know why, or what he is going to do there. He's been with this outfit eleven months and in 24 hours he is to be packed and on his way. So it goes. And then we grumble if the Captain of our Salvation sees fit to move us without consultation and our approval.

August 30, 1943 - A Typical Gospel Service

I had last night, one of the finest services I have had in the Army. I drove out to the other camp again for my evening service. Though I arrived fifteen minutes early, a good crowd had already gathered in the evening dusk. By five minutes before the appointed time of service, almost 100 men had gathered and so we began the song service. We had only about forty chairs so the others sat along the walls and some stood in groups all the way back to the door. I let them request their own songs and we sang twelve of them, two verses of each, before I finally had them sign off. I can find no organist among them so I do the playing on my field organ. I'm some musician, I tell you, but they sing so that they drown out all the mistakes. We may not be awful good but we are awful loud. I preach to them as earnest a Gospel message as I can. They are as quiet as mice. I include a number of stories of home and family. I'll never have a more attentive audience. At the close we all bow our heads in silent prayer. Then I talk to them quietly concerning Christ's call to repentance and the offer of forgiveness, peace and eternal life through the Gospel. Last night 34 men responded to the invitation. I tell you it's a sight to make angels weep for joy. We bow our knees to definitely commit them to God, give each a special edition of John's gospel, announce another service for Tuesday night and dismiss the meeting.

But the men are in no hurry to go home. At my invitation to come up and talk over any problem they may have, one after the other wait around. They come up to grip my hand. One wants to know, "Chaplain, what denomination are you? "I happen to be a Lutheran, why?" "Well," he says, "you sound like an old-time Methodist. I'm a Methodist and your message has the ring of my dear pastor at home." "Brother," I told him, "the Gospel of Christ Crucified has the same ring from men of God everywhere, regardless of their denominational badge." A Catholic lad came up to thank me for the message and to say, "I was here at your last service and God gave me such a blessing that I have brought three of my Catholic buddies with me tonight and they would like to meet you and thank you." Another big, husky farmer from Rice Lake, Wisconsin, followed me out to the truck. "Chaplain, could you possibly get in touch with my family to let them know that I am alright? I have not heard from them since last May and perhaps all my letters have been lost, too. I have a wife and two girls and I am sure they must be worried about me, as I have crossed the ocean several times." I assured him that in the morning I would get a cable off to his family through the Red Cross and within a few days they will know that he is well and safe. Then, with tears glistening in his eyes in the moonlight, he added, "It gets pretty lonely when you can't even hear from them. It gets a man down at times." "Soldier," I said, "I know. We all have our moments when the heart is sore with loneliness. But it is then we need to have faith in God. Faith, that He will safely keep and provide for those we love. Faith, that He will keep us wherever our duty calls us. Faith, that He will speedily bring this messy war to an end. Trust Him, soldier, He'll see you through. Good-night." "Good-night," he said, as he made his way off in the darkness to the long row of dark tents. It was after 11:00 p.m. when I finally got into the truck and started my long trip home. How wonderfully God had blessed the day to us. "Great is Thy Faithfulness, O Lord."

September 2, 1943

The war picture certainly looks encouraging. The Germans have just finished their worst month of the war. Her war machine is geared to summer campaigns and if she suffers reverses then, the approaching winter months look bad for her. She apparently no longer has air power to defend either her home or war front and the daily blastings are not only wrecking enormous munition plants, but workers are unable to do their work even where factories are still operating. In occupied countries, revolt and sabotage are making the job of policing, a superhuman one. It is one thing to conquer unprepared nations. It is quite another thing to make them slave for you at the point of a bayonet. Denmark is showing real spunk and will doubtless suffer terrible reprisals. Sweden will have a hard time to maintain their neutrality much longer. I pity Finland. She is in a tough spot.

However, with things cleared up in Europe, which may be not too far off, the work in the East is only begun. We cannot picture the tremendous problems of getting men and supplies into that immense Pacific area, infested with fever and disease. The Japs have had a long breathing spell in which to consolidate their gains and have worked like beavers to fortify. It will be a big job. Wonder if they'll move us over there from here? Well, one day at a time.

September 10, 1943 - JOINING THE 2nd ARMORED DIVISION

I'm on the move again! I have known it was pending for some time but, of course, we are not to indicate proposed moves in our letters so I have just had to keep this under my hat.

Today I have traveled hundreds of miles by plane. I cannot tell you what outfit I am being transferred to but I am through with the hospital. I am sending a cable just as soon as I reach my outfit to let you know I arrived safely. I am tickled over the transfer. My chief gave it to me in preference to a Captain who wanted it badly. It will be the biggest assignment I have had. May God make me equal to the increased opportunity.

I am very tired tonight and will go off to bed. My day started at 4:30 a.m. I missed my dinner and have surely covered ten miles of dusty streets in a town where I do not know a soul. But God is with me. His peace fills my soul.

September 11, 1943 - BIZERTE

I write you tonight from a ghost town. I have flown another 600 miles so I am that much closer to my destination. But here there is not a building left intact. Debris and destruction everywhere. Residents are gone, the streets are deserted except around the outskirts where troops and equipment abound.

I do have some sort of roof over my head also tonight. Also a canvas cot on which to sleep so if there is not too much air activity, I'll get some sleep.

Tomorrow I will find services to attend somewhere or find some men and have one myself.

Another couple of days and I should be with my new outfit and happy I'll be.

I am feeling fine and the Lord is with me so all is well.

September 12, 1943

I am still stranded in the ghost town but now have the happy prospect of driving most of the night by truck. That's the Army. You hang around doing nothing. Then you rush around like mad to wait some more.

But I haven't wasted my time. Besides hanging around offices by the hour trying to get instructions, I have attended a service with 650 men who have had a chance to hear very little gospel. I've visited many gruesome ruins including a ruined Cathedral. I found a Swede from New York and spoke to him about his soul. I directed three men who had just reached shore after being torpedoed last night, to a place for treatment and food. Now I am packed and ready to take off again.

September 13, 1943

After a weird ride by truck of 150 miles I arrived at our tenting place at 2:00 a.m. Half the time the driver was lost as we went meandering through the mountains. There was a full moon and the country was picturesque enough if only the roads had not been so rough and the constant strain of wondering if we would reach any signs of civilization before our gas tank went empty.

The roadsides, over much of the way, were littered with wrecked vehicles -- trucks, tanks, jeeps. Bomb craters showed up as black pits in the moonlight. We went through some of the areas of the worst fighting so it was quite an experience.

I am living in a tent again and like it. The food is quite good but the glory of it all is that we have real water. They haul it from a spring in the mountains. For once, the Army has declared it pure without ruining it with chlorine. By the time the truck gets here with it, it is quite warm but we have ways of cooling it off somewhat.

This last week it has been desperately hot here. Strong winds blowing in from the desert night and day keep it like an oven. They say it must last another week and then we can expect the fall rains. That will be a relief although we will then have the quagmire of mud to contend with.

I will have ever so many more men to work with now. You know the fine work I have been writing to you about was just about finished up. Most of the units had left the camp. Since it seemed hopeless to get anywhere with the hospital unit, I was mighty glad for a change. For them, I feel I gave my best. They have had their opportunity and I can meet them in judgment without shame, only pity.

September 14, 1943

I sat quite some time and chatted with the Swedish Chaplain last night I really like him. He knows what the new life is and I do not question that he preaches it. Then this morning a Chaplain Simpson came over. I went to Harvard and Memphis with him. He has been kicked around through a half dozen units. He never expected to be ordered overseas because his wife is an invalid and has not walked a step for three years. They have two children. He was a line officer before he became a Chaplain and has been in for about two years. He is still a Lt. Now he has malaria. Poor guy, I felt sorry for him. Then after lunch, a Chaplain Bertram came in. He is from the Missouri Synod. He's from Iowa and a fine, husky-looking fellow. He's been here since the invasion.

September 18, 1943: A Ten-Mile Hike

Yesterday I went for a swim in the indigo blue waters of the Mediterranean. There was practically no tide and no breakers. It was like swimming in a lake except for the invigorating tang of the salt water. I have never seen water as clear. Just like a picture. If only I had the movie camera now.

Today I have been for a ten-mile hike up into the mountain. I enjoy getting out by myself. The valley where we are bivouacked is flooded with water during the rainy season but there is time to raise a crop down there. The Arab farmers have their huts and gardens up in the hills round about. They really have some fine herds of cattle that certainly are imported from the U.S. But their biggest herds are goats. Herds of these are bleating everywhere through the hills. Half-grown girls and boys watch them until they see you coming and then they run for their lives. It may be they are just afraid of strangers or more likely they learned from the German occupation to keep out of the way of white men.

These days I am left to shift pretty much for myself as I have not yet been assigned to my unit. It will take several days yet. So I am using the time to write letters, read large portions of the Bible and plug away at George Elliot's "Adam Bede." She is certainly an interesting contrast with most modern novelists. Her frequent reference to Scripture, the portrayal of human virtues rather than vices and her descriptions, are unique, if at times somewhat too lengthy to sustain interest in the story itself.

It has gotten a bit cooler. In the middle of the night I have even used a blanket. Last night a regular hurricane of wind came up. I have one side of my tent rolled up all the time to get some air and believe me, I got my fill of it last night. I thought the whole thing was going to take wings. The canvas snapped and everything in the tent was moving. Needless to say, I did not sleep very well.

September 20, 1943 - We found a children's village

Have you been wondering what has become of all the little children whose homes were ruined and whose parents were killed in the war here? Well, I'll tell you about some of them.

Up on this mountain, off from the road about a half a mile, over rocks and twists and turns, we found a children's village. A missionary from Ohio who has a wife from St. Cloud and three little white-haired girls, take care of the place. They are refugees and escaped from Tunis (you can look that up on the map). In an old rattle-trap car and by mule cart, they have brought as many as 250 children, homeless, hungry and ragged, to live up here. The missionaries are Swedish people and the lady's name had been Gustavsen. Another older lady who is also a missionary and who came here thirty years ago right from Sweden, also was there. Then a man who is a Protestant Chaplain for the Free French soldiers, came in. He had come from Switzerland and was a fine Christian man. He had been a prisoner in a German camp for two months until the American troops came along and freed him.

These folks have one house and there are many tents around for the children and others. They have a large garden where they raise most of their food. They have many chickens, three donkeys and a whole herd of goats for meat and milk. They surely seemed happy up there.

After talking a while, I brought out my harp and we sang Swedish, Norwegian, French and American. The children filled the little house and joined in singing whenever it was a language they knew. The older folks stood and looked in at the open windows. Afterward I read the Bible and prayed and then the French Chaplain prayed in French. Isn't it wonderful that God understands all languages.

They told me they had not heard from America in more than six months. They have friends only one hundred miles away but it takes from six weeks to two months to get a letter to them if it does not get lost on the way. I am sure they get no money from America so I felt that Jesus wanted me to leave a missionary offering with them. Do you think it could go to any better work than that?

God has richly blessed their work among the children. They have a school for them, teach them to work in the gardens and the girls to knit and sew. They have church services and many of the children have accepted Jesus as their Saviour. Two weeks ago, on Sunday evening, 35 of them testified that they had found Jesus up there. I was so glad as we rode down the mountain that God had led me to visit them. Pray for them, won't you?

September 22, 1943 - Assigned to Second Armored Division

For me, this has been a rather exceptional day. In the first place, it has been the warmest day I have lived in North Africa. Occasionally the wind blows in off the desert (it's called a "surroco") and it is like a blast from a furnace. It blows like a tornado so the dust almost shuts out the sun and just saturates everything. I was sure my tent was coming down and there is simply no escape anywhere. I was so relieved when it finally wore itself out at about 4:00 P.M.

Then as you see by my address, I have today gotten my assignment to an outfit. F.A. stands for Field Artillery and though I have not had a chance to inspect them very much yet, I am told it is really a crack outfit with beautiful equipment. I met the commanding officer this afternoon and he seems very congenial and at least professes to be happy that I am coming and willing to cooperate. Believe me, there is some difference in the C.O. you get. As you can surmise, the outfit is close to where I've been before so I'll not be moving my quarters even for a few days.

The special reason for this is that I have also today been made Division Chaplain. Well, it is only for about two weeks as Chaplain

Nelson who has been acting division chaplain while the big shot is in Sicily, was taken to the hospital this morning. I have told you that he has been very sick since Sunday, running a temperature around 103°. They know he has dysentery and suspect malaria. So I have moved into his office and taken over. You can only see me by appointment now so be sure to send in your calling card.

September 24, 1943

Yesterday I had no time to write because it was moving day. Everything I had was loaded into a truck and off I went. In this new place we live in "Pup-tents" and sleep on the ground. We carry this little tent with us wherever we go so it is there whenever we have no other accommodations. I don't mind one bit living this way. I'd dread the idea of sleeping in a house again. So I guess we're doomed to be campers the rest of our natural lives.

This outfit has an ample supply of vehicles so I was immediately assigned a vehicle and a driver for my personal use at all times. But you could never guess what kind of a car they gave me. I have an amphibean jeep -- one of these boat affairs that goes just as well in the water as on land. In the afternoon yesterday we took it to the ocean and drove it right in. The wheels are disengaged and a propeller just like on a ship, operates the thing. It is water-tight and really is lots of fun. Now if I can get a couple of extra cans of gas and a ten-day leave, I should be able to come home for a trip. What do you say?

This morning I had another thrilling experience. I've taken my first lesson in riding a motorcycle and rode for forty miles. I've been wanting to learn to operate one of these things since I was a kid and now at last it is realized just about the time I'm getting false teeth and a bald head.

Last night I was introduced to the men of the outfit, as it was the night for the sex morality talks which we are required to give in the army every six months. Every man is there so it was really a fine opportunity. The C.O. introduced me and he certainly made some fine comments. I'm going to like it here. You know that visiting the sick was never my long suit and it was a disappointment to me when I was put in such an outfit. In a combat unit you get younger men who are friendly, often quite religious or at least look up to the Chaplain. All in all, I'm glad I'm here.

October 1, 1943 - Return to Oran on the Mediterranean

The trip is completed and I'm still writing you from North Africa. I cannot tell you much about it, of course, but will describe it in detail one day. It was really rugged, I assure you, but well worth all the trials. I have seen scenery that can well rival anything we admired in Glacier Park. I am located so close to the ocean that I can easily throw a stone from my tent into the pounding surf. In fact, this evening I can feel the spray in my face at the tent door. The constant roar of the wind and the pounding of the water will take a while to get used to, but in the army you quickly get adjusted to all the discomforts and new situations. That's one reason why they are so anxious to get young men for the service.

My face is pretty sore from the burning wind. You see, I made the whole trip in my jeep and it has no top or windshield. Every afternoon the wind starts blowing in this country. Usually it is mixed with sand. With that peppering you all day, your face feels like raw steak by night. I ought to shave tonight, but my face is so sore I cannot even rub soap on it.

Now I'm looking forward to getting in with my outfit for some real training in the field. It will be interesting I know and a fine chance to get to know my men.

October 2, 1943

Today I have had my first ride in a tank. Tomorrow I am going to drive one and one day soon I'm going to fire their cannon. We practiced roaming about in the hills all afternoon firing at targets over three miles away. It surely was interesting. As it had rained last night, the hills were very slippery but those big iron monsters get around on any kind of ground. They really ride smoothly.

Because of the kind of training an outfit like this gets, we move around a good deal and change camps very often. A change of scenery makes the days go faster and they do arrange to have time off so I can take care of my services. I like these men and like the officers better than any I have been with in the army.

October 14, 1943

I have just finished my Bible study and prayer service. We were only an even dozen, but five of these took part in prayer and participated

62

with real enthusiasm in the discussion. We are taking up the life of Christ in chronological order. Tonight we took up all the Scriptures on: 1. His pre-existence. 2. Old Testament Messianic promises. 3. His birth and childhood. Next Thursday we begin his public ministry. It will become more practical and fruitful in its spiritual application as we go along.

I am reading, after I get into my bunk at night, a rather unique book which I think I'll send you when I have finished. It is Vash Young's "A Fortune to Share." In substance, he tells of how he, a salesman full of fears, envy, suspicion, worry, discouragement, faced up to himself one day and began to "think positively instead of negatively" and it revolutionized his life. He decided that more than money or success, he wanted happiness in life. This he decided could not be found by seeking gain but in giving to others their due credit, encouragement, friendliness, etc. It has been a battle, he admits, but battles that result in victories more often than defeat. He evidently got his inspiration from reading the Bible and possibly gathered some of his strength to fight through prayer although he is not very outspoken about that. Anyway, it has brought him to where he really enjoys life, loves people, and takes one entire day in each week when he does nothing but hears peoples' troubles and tries to put them straight. It is an interesting world we live in and many are the honest, big souls that are trying to find the answers to the riddles of the universe.

I am now serving over 2,000 men and had 790 at my service last Sunday morning. It is really some thrill to speak to all of these men of the saving and keeping power of Christ. And they listen, too.

October 17, 1943

The sun is shining this afternoon and the sky is full of racing fleecy-white clouds. But about 3:00 a.m. it started to rain and I awoke, remembering it was Sunday and thought, "There goes our service." I remembered the saying of Gypsy Smith, "I have learned a long time ago that God's weather never interferes with God's work." I prayed it might be so and went off to sleep again. It was still raining when the bugle sounded off and kept it up all morning.

I had made some provision for such an emergency, however. During the week I had been after my Supply Officer to get a big storage tent put up and try to have it clear of equipment so I could use it Sunday if necessary. This he did and we went there for our service. I had arranged to have a brass quartette to play for us and they were really good. The singing was enthusiastic. Hope I can get them again. In spite of the rain, 125 men came to the service and there was just a wonderful spirit. My, it is a joy to preach to these men. Most all of them come from the south and have had at least religious homes. They are very responsive. One young fellow came after the service this morning and said, "Chaplain, I have not been going to services since I got in the army, but last Sunday you remember, they made us go and today I wanted to come. I want you to know that your sermons have meant a great deal to me and I'll be here every Sunday if I can."

October 26, 1943

I told you that your books came. I have been having a glorious time with these chorus books. Right off the bat, we learned one at our Sunday evening service:

> "Safe am I, safe am I, in the hollow of His hand;
> Sheltered o'er, sheltered o'er, with His love forevermore.
> No ill can harm me, no foes alarm me,
> For He keeps me day and night.
> Safe am I, safe am I, in the hollow of His hand."

Can you conceive of a more precious truth for men in combat? I want those who come to the service to learn it and love it so they will sing it for all our men, and I told them so.

Then I also found in those books some of my favorite solos and duets. Do you remember Homer Rodeheaver singing, "When Jesus Comes"? How I love that song. I'm going to sing it Sunday morning and had the organist over practicing it tonight.

October 30, 1943

What miracle is this that enables me in this far distant land to hear your voice speaking to me? Today I have played [daughter] Marilyn's record three times. The Base Chaplain let me go to his room where he has a phonograph radio. There all alone, I could enjoy it to my heart's content. It was almost hard to believe that I was still in this world. Marilyn chattered away just as I remembered she used to. And your voice sounded so natural.

It has turned cold here. Last night it was 40 degrees and when you are sleeping out in a tent in a damp field, you really feel it. One has little inclination to crawl out and eat your breakfast out under the stars with your teeth chattering and your food cold before it reaches your mouth. But in the midst of it all I haven't been sick a day, not even a cold. This body God has given is a wonderful machine, and really serves man for "every good work" if it is not abused. It can adjust itself to almost any hardship.

November 2, 1943 - Our Wedding Anniversary

This day is marked with red on my calendar. And well it may. For was it not on this date twenty years ago that I met under the archway of a flower-bedecked parlor in Tobson's home on Elizabeth Street, San Francisco, the bride of my choice who promised to share with me the future, for better or for worse.

Twenty years is a long time. Almost a third of the average person's life. Living as intimately as do husband and wife, one learns a great deal about the other in that time. And a great deal about oneself. The wear and tear of the daily grind bring out many unexpected quirks of character and temperament -- and not all of them flattering.

But, I trust that neither of us supposed we were marrying an angel. We were joining heart and hand with a human being with its full quota of frailties and inconsistencies. Of one thing we were absolutely certain -- we loved one another above any other mortal in this world. There is nothing that mutual love cannot correct or else bear with sympathy and understanding.

And of this love and its power, I am as confident today as then. We have had our share of pain and pleasure, sickness and health, companionship and loneliness, tears and laughs, bitter disappointment and thrilling enjoyment. And through it all, before God I assure you, I have never once honestly regretted the day I asked you to be my wife nor have I wished to be released from my lifetime pledge to you.

Now on this Anniversary, I do, in the presence of God, our Father, renew my vow made so many years ago, to love, to cherish and hold you until death do us part.

Do you remember how we planned to celebrate our 20th Anniversary? It was going to be quite an affair. Well, with the demon of war let loose in the world, all that had to be changed. But it's not cancelled, only postponed.

November 3, 1943

Today I went to headquarters and got a supply of Scriptures, Protestant, Catholic and Jewish, and then have arranged to have it announced at reveille in the morning that men who have none and wish one, I can supply them. As an added inducement, I made arrangements to get their names printed on the cover, free of charge. They will like that. Already several of the Officers have asked me for a copy. One asked if he could have the entire Bible and I was so glad to have just one copy that I could give him.

This evening I have had my Bible Class. Twenty-two came out and we were packed like sardines in my little blackout tent. We had such a wonderful time studying the new birth from John 3. We kept on for two hours and several asked questions that were really heart-searching. How I enjoy teaching the Word of God. It is indeed a mine, a garden, a storehouse. After the class, I rehearsed a couple of songs for Sunday with a chap who has a fine tenor voice and is a devout Christian. He has spent a year at Moody. We got the song, "Though your Sins be as Scarlet" worked out pretty well.

Today I have also found a bugler who can blow church call. First time in the Army that I have had such help. So now, though we have no church bell, at ten minutes before the services, he will sound off for the whole camp to hear. It's going to boost attendance I know.

I told you in the letter yesterday that I was distributing testaments to the men. In less than half of my outfit I have had eighty requests. It was thought that all of them had copies. We had special prayer tonight that God's Word might accomplish for the men what the Spirit desires.

You should see the Christmas packages pouring in here now! Bags and bags of it every day. Folks at home really got out early to shop and it's a good thing. Last year they tell me they were getting them until the last of February.

We have had rain, almost incessantly now, for three days and nights so you can imagine what this field looks like. We are fortunate that we have water-tight tents so we can keep dry at night even though your clothes are so damp in the morning they are clammy.

This week we commemorate the first anniversary of the landing of American troops on African soil. I must give the event proper recognition in the service tomorrow. It has been a year in which God has signally prospered our cause. The dawn of Liberation for many oppressed nations certainly glows much brighter today. The cost in life, energy and materials has been terrific, especially on the Eastern front and for us, the coming year will exact an even heavier toll. But sin is costly for nations as well as individuals and apparently only personal experience will teach us the lesson. May God have mercy upon us.

66

November 7, 1943 - A Vital Youth Message

Another Sunday is drawing to a close. After an entire week of rain and wind, this morning dawned as beautiful as any day I've seen. About 100 men, including 22 Officers, gathered for the morning service. I devoted some minutes at the beginning of the service to a recognition of the first Anniversary of American conquests in North Africa. Then this tenor and I sang a song and afterward I spoke on Zechariah 2:4.* There I underscored that God has a message of vital importance especially for young men -- so vital in fact, that He once sent angels to proclaim it and now has sent His servants even to follow the troops into every theatre of the war to declare it.

I. Why is He especially concerned about young men? a. Because they are inexperienced. b. Because youth is a time of strong temptation. c. Because they are essentially honest and will listen. d. Because they are important members of the community. e. Because their character will soon be fixed.

II. What does God want to tell them? a. That they have a soul to save. b. They have a life for which they must give account. c. That sin, though attractive, is costly. d. That youthful energy is intended for something more than lustful gratification. e. That there is a day of accounting coming to each of us.

We really had a blessed hour. You would be thrilled to read what these men write about the services in their letters home. I help to censor the mail and they have really been impressed. Tonight we did not have as large a turnout by far. We sang some real good choruses and I preached on "Prepare to Meet Thy God." Fourteen men asked for prayer at the close of the service and several remained for special help and prayer. God is doing a work among them, and I do praise Him for it. Whatever the future has in store for them, He is certainly giving them an opportunity now to make their peace with God.

I spent the afternoon visiting at the Hospital. We have such very limited transportation now that I could not get a vehicle. So I walked the two and a half miles each way. That only did me good.

*["And said unto him, Run, speak to this young man, saying, Jerusalem shall be inhabited as towns without walls for the multitude of men and cattle therein."]

November 10, 1943

Yesterday I visited Chaplain Harrell from Camp Hood about whom I wrote you. He really has seen some action. He landed in Africa eleven months ago, fought in Tunisia, was among the first to land at Palermo and then the first at Naples. His infantry outfit fought up through those terrific mountains where the battle is still going on. He really had a story to tell. He had been permitted to do some genuine spiritual work among the men and showed me pictures of where he had 1800 men at a service and said there were 59 definite decisions for Christ. He's a real preacher. He had been wounded several times but as they were only flesh wounds they had healed fine. He has now spent six weeks in the hospital with arthritis in both knees. He expects to be sent back to the States and I hope they send him. He says he would not want to continue over here unless he could be with combat troops and of course that cannot be.

Our good fortune is this, that our Heavenly Father has promised to guide us with His counsel. Whatever the future has in store has been first weighed out in His heart of love and apportioned as His wisdom sees best. Ours is but to rest in His will.

> "No ill can harm me, no foes alarm me,
> For He keeps both day and night."

Blessed assurance!

November 13, 1943 - "Shipping to England" on the British Ship "ORONTES"

So once again I write you from a ship stateroom. At last the move that we have anticipated and planned for has become a reality. It is hard for us to understand the value of all the time spent on this continent but anyone who thinks can realize the tremendous task and responsibility and believe me, we whose lives are the chessmen they order around, are willing to let them take their time until all possible conditions are favorable.

Well, whatever has taken place, we are in it now and will have to see it through. I need not tell you how relieved I am to leave this country and how sincerely I hope I'll not need to come back during the war or after. I have now spent almost seven months in this one theatre. During that time I have certainly had both interesting and varied experiences. I cannot question that God has wonderfully honored my humble efforts to glorify His Son. Here more than one hundred trophies of grace have been won besides the thousands who have heard the Word without manifesting any immediate change. Saints have been strengthened and local Christians and missionaries have been encouraged through our fellowship. Though I could no doubt have done so much more, I do not know myself to be guilty of conscious neglect or willful sin toward any member of the Armed Forces or the civilian population. May God in grace, overrule in any case of shortsightedness, prayerlessness or powerlessness which has made me any less than the most possible for Him in Africa. I leave, thanking Him for the trust He has given here, for the hardships, for the heartaches, for the lonely hours, too. All goes to the fulfillment of His promise in Romans 8: 28.*

I can hardly convey to you my reaction as I came into this place which is to be my home for some time if the Nazis just let it keep afloat. There are just two of us in a room that is fully 7x10. On the berth is snow-white linen, two pillows, [box]spring and mattress. I hadn't been in over five minutes before I pulled off my shoes and stretched out full length. On one wall is a dresser, on the other a wardrobe. Then we have a white wash bowl (I haven't seen one for months) and running water. The steward comes in at 7:00 a.m. to wake us and tell us our bath is ready. A real tub with hot water. Ah, me! I could lie and soak all day just with the luxury of it. It is uncanny what a thrill one gets from the ordinary things of life after having been away from them for so long.

Then comes meal-time. We eat in two shifts as the dining room is not large enough. On this ship we get three meals a day and they are really good. Spotless tables, with real china and food eaten with real silverware. I think I could even relish caster oil.

We have a lovely lounge where we can go and sit in the evenings. Usually there is too much tobacco smoke for me to enjoy it up there, but it is a very comfortable place otherwise. There's not a single woman on board but it's quite some sight to see all these tanned officers in full dress, all their brass shining.

*["And we know that all things work together for good to them that love God, to them who are the called according to his purpose."]

"Stillehavet" Not Very Still

Today is Sunday. I'd like to get a hold of that Norwegian who named this Mediterranean "Stillehavet," and teach him something about the use of words. This ship has been pitching like a bucking broncho all day. All the joints of the ship creak. Things just won't stay in place, least of all your stomach. I've had two services today. Could have had more, but did not feel quite up to it. I had fully 350 men packed into my morning service. Not quite so many this afternoon. I'll be having services every day if I'm on my feet. I'll tell you, these men listen now. They have plenty of time, of course, but mostly it is the uncertainty of what the next hour has in store that makes them reach out for refuge and security. It is a rich opportunity and I'll certainly try to make the most of it.

Still out at Sea [letter to son]

My dear Son,

Well, now the only view I have had for several days, is water everywhere. The trip has been much longer than anyone expected when we set out. But the course today is determined by enemy activity, and the reports we have received have made us quite content to spend a few extra days meandering around out on the broad expanse of the ocean.

At present the weather is grand and the ocean is very calm. But the first few days we had rough going. I spent more time than was good for me down in the hold of the ship with my men who are quartered there, and paid for it by missing one meal and failure to enjoy three others. To avoid the "Return of the swallows" you simply must get fresh air. After learning that lesson the hard way, I have now been feeling fine and really enjoy the trip.

The meals are a good deal different than what we are accustomed to but they are served well and I've been eating well. On this trip we have three meals a day. Last time we had only two.

Ready for Emergencies

We usually get up on deck for exercise in the afternoons. Several interesting and strenuous sports can be played within the narrow limits of shipboard. All the men get their daily calisthenics and inspections. In addition, we have our daily alarms and boat drills. We must constantly wear our life belts, water canteen and our water-proof flashlights. Every Officer is in charge of a group of men and responsible for launching life rafts and seeing that all his men are ready for the plunge. The flashlights are to enable him to be found in the water if we must abandon ship at night.

A big part of each day is our church service. The men really enjoy it and I usually have around three hundred present at each service. With the realization that at any moment a torpedo plane may swoop down out of a cloud to blast you to bits, it is a soul-stirring experience. Its application to life is obvious and gives rise to profitable contemplation. I have not been at all seasick since the first two days so the trip has been a joy.

Most of all, of course, do I enjoy my meetings with the men. I have been speaking to about twenty a day as I walk about the decks. So many of them now approach me first, especially the Christians. I have learned to know so many of them and share their confidences. The attendance at the services is even better this week than last in spite of the increased cold we gather out on the open deck. From 250 to 375 gather each afternoon. Ever so many have given their hearts to Christ and have sought me out to tell me so. Quite a number of backsliders have been restored. Men are asking for Bibles and stand up to publicly ask for prayer. It has been a wonderful time of refreshing and I do praise God for it.

Quartette Helps in Services

It is now 10:00 p.m. and we have just completed a quartette practice. It sounds as though we may be able to make something of it. Three of the fellows are real Christians and the fourth is not far away. They should be able to supply us with quite a few songs for the rest of the trip. It will help them spend their time profitably, too. Of course, I have not many songs arranged for male voices but one of the men is a real organist so he can arrange some of the old favorites for them.

I've had two grand services yesterday and today. About three hundred attended yesterday and about two hundred today. We had an old-fashioned testimony meeting today and a number of the men said it was the first chance they had had to give a public testimony since they got in the Army. Some of them are real genuine Christians and how glad they are to hear the gospel and the way they flock around after the service to tell me how much they enjoy it. There is not another service on the ship that compares with it. I've attended the others. They do not seem to prepare a thing and so have nothing to say. What an opportunity they are missing. These men are hungering for the truth and even the unsaved rejoice to hear it. I've won so many real friends on this boat. The Officers, too, comment on the real interest the men show and cannot quite understand it. But Christ is still the strongest magnet in the world.

***

"Fierce and wild the storm is raging,
Round a helpless bark

On to port 'tis swiftly driving,
O'er the waters dark."

I have just returned to my stateroom after a stroll about the deck. What a day! The wind is whining through the ropes and cables. The decks are awash. The rain whips your face. A pea-soup fog rests like a heavy blanket upon us and envelopes the ship. The angry water is lashed to white foam and great waves roll and pitch the ship in a ceaseless rhythm. Through it all, the mighty propellors steadily do their work of forging us ahead to our desired haven.

November 24, 1943 - ARRIVAL IN ENGLAND

(It seems that any letters I may have sent immediately after my arrival have been mislaid. It is more likely, however, that censorship regulations prevented our writing. Now the gap can be filled in.)

We had traveled fourteen days since leaving Oran, Africa. At one time we were within a few hundred miles of the harbor of New York as we maneuvered to shake off a wolf-pack of submarines which had picked up our trail. We were about eighteen troop ships in the convoy, all battle-hardened veterans. It would have been quite a prize for the Germans.

But one dark night we made our way through the Irish Sea and landed in Liverpool just the day before Thanksgiving. Though we were on a British ship (the S.S. Orontes) they were considerate enough of American customs so they did get us a small quantity of turkey for the occasion.

We lay tied up at the dock for thirty-six hours before we could unload. It was explained that we were to travel to southern England by train and no trains were available. The weather was damp with fog according to the best English tradition. There was little to relieve the monotony of waiting on shipboard. I experienced just one thrill of pleasure during this dreary waiting time and that was as I came out on the deck. I saw flying from the masthead of a neighboring ship, the Norwegian flag. It was the first time I had seen it since I left Brooklyn and it at once gave me the feeling of being much closer to my own kind than when I was in Africa.

Disembark at Night

Orders finally came for us to unload at 2:00 a.m. and swaying and grunting under the burden of baggage and equipment we made our way down the gang-plank. There were no bands playing, no enthusiasm of welcome by the English. War was real and earnest to these people and they went about their assigned tasks without emotion.

We were marched over the cobblestone pavement, through the blacked-out streets, until we arrived at the railway station. The station was dingy with soot and ill-kept. All manpower, womanpower and childpower had been harnessed to the war machine. Some Salvation Army lassies served us steaming coffee and doughnuts and rated many a cheery greeting from our boys.

We were soon stowed away in outmoded passenger coaches. There was no heat, lights or running water. We started and stopped, jerked, and started again, all night. We caught a few winks of sleep but were too crowded and uncomfortable to really rest.

The next morning we caught our first glimpse of English country life. The farm buildings looked old and substantial. The farms were small and very well cultivated. The herds of sheep and cattle looked well fed.

By evening we had reached the so-called Salisbury Plain in south-central England. The train pulled off on a siding and we were unceremoniously dumped into trucks and hauled to camp.

We were relieved beyond words to discover that we were going to spend the winter in brick barracks. Our Division was to take over an English Cavalry Camp and this was to be our home and training ground until the opening of the Second Front.

Organ Accident

I've had a tough job almost all day. When they unloaded my organ from the ship, it went overboard into the ocean. They fished it out but you can imagine the condition it was in. As it is almost new, I have tried my best to get it in working order. So today I have had it all apart. All the parts that were rusted have been polished, all that were swollen and stuck have been dried out. But I am afraid it is all to no avail. The wood is warped so I'm going to have to give up and try to get another if that is at all possible.

Tonight I have had my first session of the Bible Class. We were not many. It's funny that it always takes a few weeks to work up anything in a new place. Those who did come were thrilled. That is the most important. If those that do come get fed, they'll spread the news to others.

One of my men is painting a sign ten feet long to put up outside my Chapel. So we'll soon have the men knowing where to find us.

December 2, 1943 - Garrison Life at Tidworth, England

Now I do have an office of my own. I have two pieces of furniture: a bench on which to sit, and a table -- most essential, a cozy little fireplace at one end of the l0'xl0' room. It gets real cozy here, although the ration on coal does not allow me to keep the thing going all day. I have spent all my evenings here so far. Here the men can find me and come in to talk at any time they wish and the evening is really the only time they are free. When they are not here, I have the fine chance to read and write. I make my way home about 10:30. The other officers cannot figure out how I can endure being cooped up every night. They somehow cannot realize that I'm never alone. I visit with my loved ones and friends as I write to them. I live with the characters in my books as I read. And my unseen Friend is always so near that it seems perfectly natural to sit and talk to Him or to sing His praises.

Yesterday I called on my Senior Chaplain whom I met then for the first time. He's been away so I've never had a chance to report to him. As he welcomed me, he said, "Chaplain, I'm mighty glad to welcome you. You come with the highest recommendation and a superior efficiency rating from your last assignment and needless to say, I could not ask for more." Anything good in me, I humbly acknowledge, with Paul, can be ascribed to one thing alone: "By the grace of God I am what I am (and when I can add as he did) and his grace which was bestowed upon me was not in vain," I know it is all of Him and will be careful to give Him all the glory. But I know it helps to ease the pain of loneliness in your heart to hear that God is doing a work through me (You'll be perhaps especially interested to know that my Senior who spoke these words is a Catholic).

December 3, 1943

I've spent most of my day getting ready for Sunday. My new church has to be trimmed up. From a little town nearby, I managed to get two small bouquets of mums for the altar. They will be beautiful. They are given in memory of two of our men who have just received word that their fathers have died during the last month. Both of the men are Catholic. So today I have put in writing a note of sympathy to each and told them that the flowers are placed there in memory of their parent and that prayer will be offered for the bereaved family. As Catholics they would no doubt have preferred to have me pray "for the rest for the soul of the departed" but being a mere mortal I have no power to change the destiny of souls that have passed over the border. According to my Bible, my responsibility is toward the souls on this side of eternity. And may God give me ever a deeper concern for them.

How blessed the promises of Philippians 4:6-7.* May God help us both to practice it each day and our lives shall reflect the beauty of Jesus.

*["Be careful for nothing; but in every thing by prayer and supplication with thanksgiving let your requests be made known unto God. And the peace of God, which passeth all understanding, shall keep your hearts and minds through Christ Jesus."]

December 6, 1943

Yesterday was Sunday and I had my first services in the Chapel. My equipment has not come but I did manage to borrow some song books and a folding organ from the Salvation Army. I had gotten the heat working so it was comfortable. The lights we also managed to get connected up. My organist was a chap who has been assistant to my predecessor and consequently expects to be mine. His chief qualification for the assignment is his nineteen years of experience as musician for dance orchestras and on the vaudeville stage. (He very earnestly confided in me yesterday that he wanted nothing to do with this Fisherman's Group because they were a bunch of fanatics.) Isn't life interesting?

After the service a chap introduced himself to me as Willy Bjornstad. He's from Underwood, just a mile from our place there. Now he is a Christian and worked for some time with the American Sunday School Union. I invited him up to my office afterward.

December 9, 1943 - Rain as Usual

While the officers are having their party and dance, I have a fine chance for a little chat with you. I might start off by telling you it's been drizzling all day but that's no news in Britain this time of year. It seldom does anything else but. We're equipped with three buckled rubber overshoes. Then we wear our steel helmets and good raincoats. So we're well protected.

Last night I had no chance to write because one of our companies went out on a march and, of course, I went along. We travelled by compass across fields, slushing through the mud and water. We walked about six miles. When I got home, I took a detour by the mess hall. The cooks were busy preparing a swell breakfast for the men. I was treated to hot coffee, three baking powder biscuits, french-fried potatoes and a hamburger left over from supper. That really put me in swell shape. I went home and slept like a log.

All of my equipment has finally come so I've been busy today unpacking, arranging a tract table in the Chapel and then spent all afternoon getting out my report for last month.

The tea party with the Chaplains Monday night was a very pleasant affair. They served coffee instead of tea. The British Army has compulsory church attendance but where they are free to choose it is reported they are less responsive than our own troops. It's a debatable question as to which is the better system.

I didn't get too much sleep last night as another Army party was on. Really, they were quite proper, though. I do not believe that a one of them had over a couple of drinks of beer. They quit dancing promptly at midnight. Then they had to take the women home and that is no joke as they have to drive in complete black-out. They all go in a group and use a truck. They didn't get back until 2:00 a.m. But breakfast was served at the usual hour. At 8:00 a.m. every unit checked to see that every man was on the job and if not, he had to report to headquarters and really take a tongue lashing. I really think it pretty fine that they do not allow men to be fooling around so it interferes with their work.

December 26, 1943 - CHRISTMAS EVE IN ENGLAND

First we had to get to work in the Chapel. It is a very cold and drab place with a floor of tarred paving blocks, walls of rough brick and sky-lights in the ceiling which must be kept covered with blackout curtains.

I managed to buy a tree in a town nearby, for $4. It was really a pretty thing. Then I wanted to build an altar-rail at which men can kneel in our after meetings and communion services so they do not have to get down on that hard, cold floor. Well, I found some lumber from packing crates in which our guns had been shipped, found a hammer and saw, and managed to nail together a very presentable altar. Then we went to a store-room and found some clean burlap bags. These we ripped and covered the altar, padding the kneeler and top.

Next we tackled the tree. A box filled with dirt formed the support. The tree is awkward to handle because it has a number of roots to it. You see, they must be planted again. They claim that 70% of them will grow again after the holidays. I tried in three towns and the Red

Cross to get some decorations. But that was simply out of the question. I couldn't even buy one sheet of colored paper to make things out of. So what to do, what to do? But the ideas began to come. I went to the dispensary where I got a large roll of cotton and a couple of boxes of epsom salts. The cotton we made into little flakes which we spread over the tree (it is the only white Christmas we had this year) and a few grains of epsom salts made them sparkle very realistically. My only bed sheet I put over the box at the bottom of the tree. Then I collected about 20 beautiful Christmas cards, punched a hole in one corner, put through a string and tied them on the tree. I had found four wreaths of holly with red berries and a few small pine branches with cones. With these we trimmed the chancel and along the altar we spread evergreen branches. Finally I went to our radio section and got a large sheet of tin foil which they use for conductors or something, and made a large star at the top of the tree. An electrician found me a wire extention and a globe so crowned the tree with the star.

By 3:00 p.m. on Christmas Eve it was all ready. And it looked so nice that as I sat there alone and looked, a lump came into my throat and tears dimmed my eyes as I thought of you all. And I prayed that God would give you all a very blessed Christmas.

Then I had to be on my way. From a church nearby, we had set up a broadcasting system where the chaplains have been sponsoring programs of Christmas carols all week. This was my day. I took my organist with me and between numbers on the church organ and records, we kept going until 5:00 p.m. While we sat there, a soldier, very obviously quite drunk, came in and said, "Chaplain, may I stay and listen to the organ? I was lying in my bunk and heard the music and just followed it up here. It reminded me of my mother. She used to play like that." He sat through the broadcast and as we left I had a chance to speak to him about Christ and his home. He wept as I told him that he would never go very far wrong if he just kept remembering his dear mother at home waiting for him and that he must never do anything that would bring shame upon her.

Then it was time to get an early supper and get ready to leave camp. I felt that many of the men would be quite lonely, especially on Christmas Eve. I knew that I would be. That was always our night with our little family and to sit and think about that here would be just too much, so I had arranged to take a group with me out Christmas caroling in a town 20 miles away. I had secured permission from the British police to drive around the streets with the men and sing. Then I had been invited to bring my choir to the officers Red Cross Club and also to the Enlisted Mens Club.

We took off at 7:00 p.m. Have you ever tried to drive 20 miles in the fog at night without lights? It's no joke and, of course, here we must always drive without lights. It took us just one hour and 45 minutes. So we pulled up at the Officers' Club just before 9:00 p.m. The dance band was just getting tuned up but the director of the club told us to go ahead. So we borrowed the microphone and announced what we were there for, then distributed song sheets to all present and invited them to join us on certain verses or, if they preferred, they could just listen. I think there was not an officer or his lady friend who did not join us. We do not have a regular choir, but I had practiced with these men in seven rehearsals and they really did well. Between songs I read portions of God's Word to bring out the message and in my greeting at the close, I had a chance to speak a few words for Christ. So many of the officers spoke to me their appreciation and I feel it was a real opportunity to bear witness for Christ. A member of the dance orchestra said, "This was swell. I haven't sung these songs in a long time. I'd rather go with your men tonight than stay here and play the saxophone."

So we packed our folding organ and books and loaded into our 2½ ton truck again. We took off the canvas top and with the little organ playing we made off slowly down the street singing as we went. Faces peered out from behind black-out curtains at the windows. Others stood in doorways and shouted a merry Christmas as we passed. And before long we had a large group walking on the sidewalks and out in the streets beside the truck, joining in the song. And all of this in inky blackness except for the faint glow of small flashlights which everyone carried. It was a soul-stirring sight.

At 10:15 we pulled up at the enlisted men's Red Cross. Through the crowd at the door, we pushed our way in and we were soon singing for and with a crowd of 1500. Again we read the Christmas story and brought a brief greeting. Needless to say, our voices were so completely used up toward the last that there was not the clearest melody or harmony.

We finished off here by being invited to a hall upstairs where they fed us hot coffee and cream puffs and then we started out once more for home. We pulled into camp at 1:15 a.m. after what everyone agreed was the grandest Christmas Eve they'd had in the Army.

Part II: 1944

January 1, 1944 - NEW YEAR'S EVE IN ENGLAND

It is New Year's Day, 1944. Ever since this morning the sun has been bravely trying to make its way through the clouds to bring light and cheer into the new year that is born. What tremendous changes this year is going to make for the entire world and for coming generations. So many questions, that directly affect so many millions of lives will be answered in 1944. It is undoubtedly the most crucial year in our generation. How glad I am to know that the entire unknown future is known to the One who said, "I will guide thee with my councel and afterward receive thee to glory."

In telling you the news, I must start with last night. I had worked so hard during Christmas and with the plans for this day and the Sunday which follows with services tomorrow and then added to all that, having a cold which I'm just managing to keep licked; I just didn't feel equal to planning anything for New Year's Eve. But as the day approached I began to feel a bit uneasy about not being able to gather with God's people at such a time. I was therefore very happy when another Chaplain dropped in to say that he had been invited to conduct a devotional service at a Baptist Church in the town where we spent Christmas Eve. He invited me to go along and when I accepted, he asked that I bring the message and he lead the service. We loaded up some 45 men in two trucks and took off at 7:00 p.m. At the church we found about 75 folks gathered. Most of them were young women (many in the uniform of the seemingly numberless branches of women's military services) and about a dozen old folks and several U.S. troops. Having heard of how folks were planning to spend the evening in various wild gatherings, my soul thrilled as soon as I came in, to realize there are still many young people who choose to come together in the church of God at such a season and prefer good talk, good fun, good singing and a good gospel to filth and debauchery. We were made welcome and our men soon joined in the games, all of which were enthusiastic and altogether wholesome. The old folks sat around and enjoyed it, too. By 10:00 p.m. they took time out for refreshments. There was a surprisingly fine variety of pastries and tea. At 11:15 we started our service. Everyone gladly joined hands in a circle and sang, "Blest be the Tie," and then I closed with prayer. At 12:15, and after many thanks to these good people who had opened their church and hearts to us, we hit for home through the night. One observation impressed me this evening as we reached home at 1:30. Here I had driven forty miles, spent the whole evening in a large town and now back at camp, and I had not seen one single drunk person all evening. Praise God! And then today I read in my paper that the city of New York was expected to spend three million dollars for one night's debauchery. Our beloved America has so much yet to learn. God is so patient with us.

At any rate, I was so grateful for the President's proclamation that this day be a day of prayer and we had made every possible arrangement to take full advantage of it. I told you of the large prayer service we had arranged. All who wished to attend were excused from duty. About 750 were present. It was quite an inspiration.

But realizing the thousands we would not reach in this way, I had asked my colonel's permission to go to every mess hall (dining hall) and speak a few words and lead them in prayer. This he agreed to. So after our large service, I went to the Mess where I called them all to attention, told them the meaning of this day, reminded them of the crucial days ahead, and invited them to join me in spirit as I led them in prayer. Every man removed his helmet and I didn't hear a sound. Not all of them eat at the same setting, so this had to be done three times. Thus I met 1400 men with this vital message. I had also asked permission to do the same at the officers mess and got the permission. Some of them, I suppose, will not be able to enjoy a meal for a month at the thought that they had to listen to a prayer but the majority were truly reverent and felt it very appropriate. Regardless of what they think, it is still right.

I finally got my own dinner and for every man here, it was another real feast.

January 7, 1944 - Visiting the Norwegian 99th Infantry Battalion

One of our Chaplains came in to report that he had just met a Chaplain in which he knew I'd be interested. It turns out that he is the chaplain of the outfit you may remember I was anxious to get into a year ago when we drove to the Mission Meetings. Remember? They are close to me here and I'm going to try to look them up tomorrow. I understand a number of the fellows know me and come from home. So I am real excited about it.

At 4:00 p.m. I took off to find the outfit of which I wrote to you last and located it just about a mile away. The first chap I ran into was Lt. Nesvig. He is the son of Rev. Nesvig at Stoughton, Wisconsin, where I had meetings once. His mother is one of the Ostrom's from Canada. He helped me contact others that I knew. I found a Klukken boy from Bellingham and a Tornquist lad from Bethany in Brooklyn. Also Bjarne

Nyborg who led the Young People at 52nd Street Church. He is doing the same in this outfit. We had a swell time chatting for an hour. Then I met the Chaplain who was very friendly.

I got the whole story of the outfit from him. I certainly have had a much richer opportunity for service than if I had gotten into that outfit. Just another proof of how God chooses the very best for those who leave the choice to Him. Then they told us that Chaplain Carlson was coming to visit them on Sunday night, so of course I had to make arrangements to come back.

February 2, 1944 - A Furlough in London

I've just finished my dinner of soup, salad, roast lamb, mashed potatoes, brussel sprouts and creamed rice. I've eaten at the Red Cross and here I have also gotten a room for my stay. Three officers occupy the room. Single beds, grand mattresses, fresh linen, plenty of windows to open, a grand bathroom with both tub and shower. All in all I have the makings of a grand vacation.

I came down with two other officers but of course they want to stay where they can get Waldorf-Astoria service and can have drinking and parties all night, so they would not think of a place like this. So we just went each our own way and everyone is happy.

When I arrived this afternoon I spent about three hours cleaning up. I soaked in the tub, shaved, brushed my teeth, polished my shoes, and got all dolled up -- for who? Nobody. It just feels grand to really get away from grime, mud and army camps for a little while.

I'm really doing very well as a man of leisure. I've managed to leave all my work behind and relax. I've been getting in about 10 hours of sleep a night in a very comfortable and clean bed. Occasionally one is very rudely interrupted by air raids but when the thunder and shock are over I go right off to sleep again. I don't think I've ever known any real fear of raids and if I did, it's worn off by now. It's just one of those things about which you take reasonable precautions and then rest satisfied that, being in the will of God, not even a shrapnel reaches you unless He permits it. It's a mighty carefree life. The blessings of the presence of God become more precious daily.

I Meet an American Nurse

I've run into one person I know. An American nurse came running up to me right downtown yesterday to ask, "Pardon me, but are you not Pastor Walstad?" I had to admit that I was but I could not place her at all. It develops that she is Sophie Ryan from Grand Forks. She was in town for just a day and we talked for about an hour. She had been at the Mission Meetings when I spoke of my work in the Army and it was there that she had gotten her vision to join up. She is a genuine Christian, apparently the only one in her outfit. We had prayer together before she left and she was very earnest.

February 6, 1944 - The Spiritual Picture

The spiritual picture of Britain is not bright. Massive churches stand practically empty. They are steeped in tradition, ornate with breathtaking splendor, solemn with ritual and liturgy. But where is the cheering, contagious, life-giving sweetness and beauty, the vigor and vitality of Christ and His spirit? It's gone.

Besides London, I spent a day in Colchester up the coast where I stayed at the Headquarters of the Worldwide Evangelization Crusade. The folks were friendly and I made some fine contacts with British and Canadian service men at a service where I spoke.

Ingrid Larsen of Brooklyn, was unable to get to London, so I arranged to go by her camp on my way home. She had arranged for me to stay at a British home about half a mile from her camp. It certainly was a joy to see her. She looks good in her uniform. I arrived in the afternoon and she had arranged for these folks to have dinner for me. I cannot explain to you how I enjoyed that meal. I had roast chicken and french-fried potatoes, home-made rye bread, two kinds of sweet rolls, jelly, A WHOLE PITCHER OF REAL MILK, and pie. You know, I have not tasted milk for 10 months. It almost seemed too wonderful to swallow it.

Ingrid went on night duty at 7:00 p.m. so a doctor was my host for the evening. I spent the night at his home in a swell bed and slept until 8:30 a.m. For breakfast I had crisp graham toast and two fresh boiled eggs. When I left the lady prepared two sandwiches for the train and then added two home grown apples. Eggs or apples I have not tasted in months. Words just could not describe my gratitude to these good people.

They had a piano so I sang a number of songs for the parents and their two children, ages 4 and 7 years.

Ingrid got up an hour before I left so we had time to speak about spiritual things and had a blessed season of prayer. She is living wonderfully close to God and the testimony of all her unsaved associates about her, makes your heart rejoice.

Right here I must mention what you wrote of in your letters which awaited me upon my return, concerning the worldly atmosphere in which you find yourself and the trials of being alone. Do you know that this is just what many of these real Christian nurses are up against in the army all through the year? There seldom seems to be more than one Christian among them. They live in large barracks with girls who seem to try to outdo one another in ungodliness. Some of them seem to delight in making life as miserable as possible for the Christians -- especially is this true of the women. A Christian may go all day long without a soul speaking a civil word to her, but she must stay on, live, work, and eat with them for the duration. We must pray much for them that they shall not become discouraged. For only as they are rejoicing in the Lord and find His companionship sufficient for all the lonely hours, will they be able to live and witness so as to win others.

So when you feel your surroundings are uncongenial and your opportunities for worship and fellowship are few, remember your many fellow Christians who these days are facing the same trial. "And God is able to make <u>all</u> grace abound toward you so that ye <u>always</u> having <u>all</u> sufficiency in <u>all</u> things may <u>abound</u> to <u>every</u> good work." Praise God.

February 14, 1944 - Work for God in Garrison

Since starting this letter, I have had the joy of leading a soldier to Christ. He is the champion middleweight boxer of our outfit, a peach of a fellow. He was at the service last night when I spoke on "After death, What?" He said he has not been able to get it out of his mind and though he has been desiring for some time to become a Christian, he just had not felt equal until now, of facing the test of a separated Christian life. It was a glorious moment, as with tears streaming down his cheeks, we knelt here in my little office and he yielded himself wholly to Christ. This is our crown of rejoicing and exceeding great reward.

It seems our service on Sunday caused quite a sensation. The full Colonel who is over all three of my outfits, was at the service for the first time. He is an old West Point man and hard as nails, of course. He has made it rather embarrassing for some of the Chaplains here so it was not at all certain what his reaction would be. I stood at the rear of the Chapel, as always, and greeted all who were there. He said, "That was a fine sermon, Chaplain; I'll see you later." Afterward I was told by one of my officers that he had asked, "Does the Chaplain always preach like that?" The officer said that we always had fine services, but that this morning was undoubtedly one of the best. Later I met the Colonel at Headquarters and he said, "Chaplain, that was a great sermon this morning. I wish that there were some way to get every man in camp to hear it." Several days since, many men and officers have been telling me what a blessed message it was. Today a captain told me, "I understand that I really missed something by over-sleeping Sunday. Come in and wake me in time to get to church this Sunday, will you?" Well, it is interesting to see that the things of God can make a dent in all the worldliness of an army garrison so that even high ranking officers must take notice. May God continue to grant the Holy Ghost-power and direct my every step.

* * *

I was especially encouraged by the turnout today because I have just had quite a discussion this week with a high ranking officer who said that the only way to win the cooperation and good-will of the officers in the army is to be one with them in their social life and all. He assured me that it was the wrong psychology entirely to be as stand-offish as I was. But God is the defense of those who obey Him. I had 109 men at the service this morning in spite of the tough training period through which we have passed. There were 15 officers present. This afternoon I talked with one of the Christian men who belong to an outfit where the Chaplain is young and a likable "mixer." I know that he was at the dance last night, being a good fellow, but he had eight at his service this morning.

March 10, 1944 - Marriages Among Army Personnel

I had perfectly good intentions of spending a good share of this evening writing to you, but to paraphrase: "A Lieutenant proposes but the General disposes." So I find myself at bedtime just having been released from an officers' school about which we heard nothing until we sat down at the supper table. So for three hours now I've been sitting in a room hazy with tobacco. Even so, perhaps it's not so hard on me as on those men who make dates and cannot keep them. It must be pretty rough to mix romance and war.

In spite of the difficulties, however, some of them seem to make remarkable progress. One of our Captains is marrying an American nurse next week whom he met for the first time after landing here.

That brings up another interesting thing. No American Chaplain is allowed to perform marriages here. Not even among our own troops. The local English clergy must officiate. In a way it's a relief. I'm glad I need have nothing to do with these wartime marriages resulting from a courtship of a few months. But it is, nevertheless, quite a disappointment to many of the couples where the Chaplain has probably been with them ever since they entered the service and then they must go to a complete stranger to have the ceremony.

The army, of course, does a good deal to discourage marriage overseas. It requires long waiting (usually three months) while application and investigations are made and approval is <u>sometimes</u> granted. All the legal angles, the immigration complications involving citizenship, the getting of the wife to America after the war; these are a few of the matters that must be thoroughly considered and understood. Well, I'm glad my courting days were over before I came overseas and my marital status settled for life!

March 21, 1944 - Lutheranism in England

This is the first day of spring. Here it has been a raw, cold day with the mist occasionally turning to showers. The trees are budding, though, and I have seen large patches of gorgeous crocuses. The grass has been green all winter so little change is noticeable.

I'm in the big city, London, again on business. Have been buying some beautiful velvet hanging for the altar in my chapel. Tomorrow I'm getting it hemmed, pleated and hooks sewed in and then I hit for camp. (Esther Fuglestad did the work for me.)

Besides this deal, I have today taken a three-hour session of Lutheran Chaplains and clergymen. It proved a disappointment except for the people I met. It was a terribly long way out into the suburbs but I found it in a dingy, drab neighborhood.

Did you know England has no English-speaking Lutheran church? The only congregations are some foreign speaking groups: German, Norwegian, Finnish, Swedish. The Missouri Lutheran have sent a pastor over from the States to try and work up something in English and to provide for the thousands of military personnel who come here on leave. I cannot imagine a less satisfactory set-up to attain the goal. This group cannot even give communion to any other Lutherans than their own. God help us. Then they have located themselves miles from down-town where the troops, hotels and Red Cross Clubs are. What a pathetic mission enterprise.

Three German refugee ministers, each of whom have small congregations here, were present and ten Chaplains with the Lutheran countries in the grip of Naziism, with thousands of their countrymen in our land as prisoners of war, they had chosen to devote the day's Conference to a discussion on the "Differences in the views of Lutheran Clergy on the Inspiration of the Scriptures as held by American and

European Clergy." Hair-splitting definitions, theological abstractions, philosophical interpretations, wearied the mind and left the soul empty. If that's the kind of a spiritual diet Germany has been fed these last decades, then it is no wonder there was no spiritual power to stem the tide of Hitlerite paganism.

America has something to learn from the spiritual decadence of Britain and Europe. Orthodoxy and evangelism must go hand in hand. Growth in knowledge and in grace -- heart and head. Revival fervor with genuine Biblical scholarship. Unless Holy Ghost fire can vitalize our theology, it is so much chaff. And chaff is a mighty poor diet for souls drying up in a world of materialism. I wish I were just starting out in the ministry.

[April 9] Easter Sunday 1944 in England

This is Easter. My second one overseas. A day associated with so many heart-warming memories from you and home. I think of the lovely breakfast which you always prepared. And then of all the neatly ironed clothes, carefully laid out for the children. Even in our perpetual shortage of money, you usually managed to be wearing something new that day. Then off to the church where, among the throngs that gathered, my heart would swell with pride as I looked down at our family seated all clean, happy and healthy.

My day started today with a sunrise service which drew a tremendous crowd (estimated 11,000 men). Others besides ourselves took part and it was an inspiring and worthy commemoration of the day.

After this service, we returned for breakfast. No Easter eggs this year, either. But it was a definite improvement over last year when I ate from a mess kit off the tail-end of a truck. We had tomato juice, cereal, french toast, bacon and coffee.

At 10:00 we had an out-door service in our own area. It was well-planned and worked out beautifully except -- the weather. It had been cold and overcast at the first service. By the time we had gotten ten minutes into our second one, it began to mist and I soon found myself standing and preaching with the rain running down my face. Well, we are field soldiers so there was no harm in getting a bit wet. I cut my sermon quite short but we had our special singing and finished off in an orderly manner.

Yesterday I had a real thrill. You remember Robert Lund from 59th (a blond giant). He's stationed about 70 miles from here and had driven over in a jeep just to spend a few hours with me. He looked grand and has put on weight. He has been getting ahead, too, as he is now a

Warrant Officer and looks real classy in his blue uniform with gold braid. He had supper with me, I showed him the camp and the pictures I have and then they took off for home about 9:30. I had to study until midnight to make up for it, but it was really worth it.

This afternoon the sun is out in all its Easter glory. A breeze like a caressing zephyr waves the grass. Daffodils are in full bloom along the wall of our barracks. Colorful crocuses peep out everywhere. The birds warble their welcome to spring.

So amid the roar of bombers overhead and the thundering bursts of artillery fire, God keeps reminding us that though the man-made world is in distress because of sin, God's world is one of harmony, joy and song. When nations shall have learned what things belong unto their peace, men shall be free and glad again.

April 18, 1944 - Preparations for Invasion

It is 10:00 p.m. and I have just finished two class periods since supper. These subjects (the nature of which I may not describe) are fascinating but pretty difficult for me. They even are too much for some of these artillerymen who have done nothing else for the past ten or twenty years. So when they joke about me missing one of them, I just fire back, "O.K.? When we get through with this exam I'll give you one in theology and then we'll see who laughs at who." We have a lot of fun. But it does take a great deal of my time as there are books and books to read on the subject. Until I joined this outfit, I had no need for this instruction but here it is indispensable so I'll keep plugging away at it.

You express surprise at the amount of studying necessary for combat. I was surprised, too. I had pretty much the idea that you go out there and pull the trigger and that is that. Actually, artillery is a very technical and mathematically involved business. It requires a thorough knowledge of higher mathematics. All the officers are college graduates who have specialized in this. But even for them, continual study is necessary for new weapons are always being developed with new gadgets. War today is desperately scientific and requires real brain power.

You ask if the soldiers do not become anxious in the midst of all this preparation. It is strange, but a fact proven over and over, that the average man has very little appreciation of the dangers of combat. He knows that thousands will be killed. He knows he may be one of them. But somehow it doesn't register in the sense of worrying him. This constant dealing with deadly weapons for years as these men have, seems to do away with the shock of possible or even probable death. The only thing that really gets them down is to be doing nothing. It is then we have problems of discipline, etc. As training steps up, they take interest, do their job, are in good spirits and take hardships cheerfully.

May 19, 1944 - Mother's Day 1944

I think I haven't told you about our Mother's Day services. They turned out just grand. I knew we would not have room in our chapel so I asked permission to use the theatre and that was granted. We fixed it all up with our altar hanging, altar, communion set, pulpit and two large bouquets of flowers: violets, tulips, lilacs, irises and another kind of which I do not even know the name. The service was announced for 10:00 a.m. At 9:30 I began playing hymns over the loud speaker. Immediately, men started coming to the service and by ten we had 415 men there, including 27 officers. It was a most impressive service and men were more deeply moved than I have seen them in a long time.

In the evening we had a second Mother's Day service and had the great joy of seeing twelve men come to Christ. Can you imagine any finer commemoration of the day than that these men shall answer mother's prayers and respond to the Saviour's love? One especially told me, "Chaplain, I now want to ask you to write to my mother. My life has been utterly without God but tonight I'm beginning a new life. I want her to hear it from you as well as from me."

A Man Opens his Heart

And now since I wrote that last sentence, a man has been sitting here for an hour telling me his troubles. His sister who is 65 and as dear to him as a mother, is at home sick with cancer and must die within a few months. Added to this, her husband to whom she has been married for over twenty years, has divorced her and she is left destitute. The soldier is forty years old and has lung trouble. First he wants me to write to his dear sister to help prepare her to die. Then he wants me to try to get a discharge for him from the army. He has with him two letters from his wife which I must sit and read. He has been married 17 years and she certainly loves him. He looks like a fine fellow. He says he is not a Christian, but his wife is. Well, well. Not much can be done about the discharge unless I can get the medics to work for it. The letter to his sister will be work for another couple of hours. And so my days go. No monotony. No time to waste.

Oh, I wanted to tell you another thing about Sunday. I told you I had visited the Mueller Orphan Homes at Bristol. It occurred to me that it would be a good thing for these fellows on Mother's Day to give a little to those hundreds of children who have never had a home or a mother's love. I announced it at the services and placed a basket down by the door for anyone who wanted to give. What do you think came in -- no less than $250.00! Wasn't that wonderful? Monday morning I obtained permission to fly by plane up to deliver it. The treasurer whom I had met before, was not in, but I explained to another gentleman about the offering. He was mildly interested. I suppose he expected five or six dollars. So I pulled the check out of my pocket and handed it to him. He almost fainted. I have since gotten a receipt and a fine letter of appreciation.

Another event of interest on Sunday night was that I received one of my men into membership into his Methodist Church. I received from a Methodist Chaplain the vows that they require and then read them off, had the man answer and then we kneeled together at our altar, prayed, and ended the little ceremony by extending to him on behalf of his home church, the right hand of fellowship. It was really very impressive and will undoubtedly cause others to think, too.

Now I must sign off and get all shined up for a formal parade. We must have those occasionally, you know. So it's good-bye for now.

May 29, 1944 - Our Last Sunday in England

Another week-end has come and gone. In every respect it was a perfect day. The weather was like mid-summer; clear as crystal and really hot. We started our broadcast of church music at 9:30. At 9:50 the bugler blew "Church Call" from two hilltops. By ten, men were streaming into the chapel in droves. We carried in every extra bench we could find and opened the doors wide. Every available place was taken. It was a real thrill to face them -- 275 men. A male quartet sang "At the Cross" and I spoke on "Overcomers." By way of introduction I said I did not question the outcome of the military conflict. But when we have won the global war, will you have won? In other words, while you're successfully fighting the enemy across the channel, are you being defeated in your personal battle with sin? I said it is possible for us to come out of this thing with our minds warped by hate, morals degraded so we no longer distinguish right from wrong and our souls bankrupt by forgetfulness of God. But it need not be so. We can be OVERCOMERS. How? The secret is

1 John 5:3-5.* It was a mighty solemn hour and many a man sat very uncomfortable.

*["For this is the love of God, that we keep his commandments: and his commandments are not grievous. For whatsoever is born of God overcometh the world: and this is the victory that overcometh the world, even our faith. Who is he that overcometh the world, but he that believeth that Jesus is the Son of God?"]

A Spiritual "Blackout"

In the afternoon I went out for another service to my old outfit from Texas. My, one can certainly see the effect of lack of religious interest on the part of the C.O. and of no regular Chaplain. Not more than thirty men came out. I spoke on "Blackout." I underscored that it was not so serious that street lights were blacked out. That which is really important is that war shall not black out in our souls faith, hope and love (I Corinthians 13:13).

June 3, 1944 - ON THE EVE OF THE INVASION, England

I have not really gotten much done today. It has been a Monday like so many in the States after a very strenuous Sunday. One just feels all done up and there is no use trying to do much of anything. But I did prepare my sermon for tonight. I spoke on Psalm 139:1-5. It was such a blessing to the men. Afterward one of the men went out and got one of his barracks mates and brought him in. It develops that he had been coming to the chapel for three nights after others had gone to bed and praying to God to save him. Tonight he has not only sought but has "found" and has gone on his way rejoicing. What a glorious way to close the day. God has been so good to us here. Many are the trophies of grace He has won and many will in days to come speak of this machine-gun range as the place where they were born into God's Kingdom.

And God has been so good to me, too. Through His power I have been enabled to live Christ so as not to bring reproach upon His name or sorrow to His children. How wonderful that God can enable weak clay to stand firm against the flood of ungodliness. Most certainly my life has been far from perfect but I can say to His glory that I have preached the whole counsel of God and have lived so that I am free from the blood of these men. Many have rejected Him but we have done what we could.

Now we face the future, holding high the banner of the cross, with victory in our souls and a song in our hearts. God is our all-sufficient helper in every hour of need. Never was there a time in life when it meant so much to be a Christian.

June 7, 1944 - THE SECOND FRONT:
Somewhere in France

I do hope this letter hurries along its way. I know so well with what suspense you have been waiting to hear after the abrupt silence several days ago. No doubt you have fully anticipated that I would be among the first to leave. For me, it was terribly hard knowing all along when my last letter would be sent and yet being unable to hint a word about it.

Well, as you see, your vagabond husband has now reached another country and another continent. I hasten to say that I am perfectly well. Right now I'm sitting under a tree trying to get these lines sent off to you with the deafening roar of heavy artillery splitting the air and every conceivable type of aircraft zooming overhead. But you must not feel sorry for me. I'm just fine and somehow one even learns to concentrate under these adverse conditions. I'll wager I will have no more typographical errors in this letter than those I used to write from my office.

You will understand, of course, that so many things you would like to hear and that I would like to write about, cannot be told at this time. They will belong to those nights we sit together by the fire and chat by the hour. But I can say that we made the crossing without mishap. Not all were so fortunate. We were subjected to three raids and the flak rained on the ship like hail but there were no casualties. In the short time we were on shipboard I had two services, one a preaching and prayer service and the other a communion service. In addition, I was given the use of the ship's loudspeaker to lead all troops in a prayer of thanksgiving for our safe journey. I was the only Chaplain on board this time. How wondrously near God is in every time of special need. The special promise He gave me for the journey was Isaiah 41:10-13.* In the strength of this word my soul enjoyed abundant peace and I had a glorious sense of assurance concerning the outcome of this conflict.

The campaign thus far is going well. We expect much more serious counter-attacks shortly but we also will have so much more to meet them with. Even if I could tell you, you could never visualize the almost limitless flow of man-power and equipment which is being brought over every hour of the day and night. History has never witnessed anything to compare with it. The organization and co-ordination is something to marvel at. Every detail of our protection, weapons and food has been carefully worked out and we are not suffering.

Casualties on both sides have been amazingly light but will no doubt become heavier as more and more units gets involved. We have taken quite a number of prisoners. I cannot but note the contrast between these and the ones taken in Africa. A large percentage of these are mere children. Others are much too old for combat duty. After only two days of fighting, I saw two of them carrying a five-gallon can of water and they almost fell on their faces with it. Most of their uniforms are in sorry condition. Obviously, the pick of Germany's man-power has been wiped out. Now vast numbers will have to try to make up for the lack in efficiency and stamina. They certainly did not look like supermen to me. A great number of them are being shipped every few hours to Britain.

I hope you keep some good papers of the first days of the invasion. We do not have papers, we do not get radio news and all we know about the progress being made is our little sector and the wounded with whom we speak who are brought in from other areas. It will be interesting to see how the newspaper accounts tally with eye-witness observations.

*["Fear thou not; for I am with thee: be not dismayed; for I am thy God: I will strengthen thee; yea, I will help thee; yea, I will uphold thee with the right hand of my righteousness. Behold, all they that were incensed against thee shall be ashamed and confounded: they shall be as nothing; and they that strive with thee shall perish. Thou shalt seek them, and shalt not find them, even them that contended with thee: they that war against thee shall be as nothing, and as a thing of nought. For I the LORD thy God will hold thy right hand, saying unto thee, Fear not; I will help thee."]

Impressions of France

France is a beautiful country. My work requires me to drive about a good deal from one unit to another and I have already seen a good deal of this sector. About all we have heard of France, you know, is Paris with its night life, godlessness and filth. Actually, the very large majority of Frenchmen are home-loving, pious, quaint and industrious.

Even thousands of those who live in the cities have a little farm which is their pride and to which they go on week-ends and in the summer as much as possible. Every family feels that they must own a bit of land. Hence the countryside is all squared off like a checker-board with little fields of three or four acres. Vineyards and orchards are everywhere. Gardens are well kept and flowers grow in abundance. Around each field there is a high, thick hedge, most often interspersed with berry bushes. Herds of the sleekest cattle I have ever seen graze everywhere. It is sad to see the many fine cattle and horses that have gotten in the way of shells or have stepped on land mines. Today I saw a cow lying dead and bloated. Alongside her was a beautiful little calf only about two weeks old. Men said they had seen it there yesterday too. Tragic little victims of man's beastiality. I would like to have gone and chased it off rather than have it lay there and pine. But if you want to keep your head on, you just do not go around inspecting or even doing kind deeds. The probability is that the Germans in retreat have planted mines about these areas, as thick as flies. So you curb your curiosity, you grit your teeth at all the wanton destruction of life and go ahead with your job.

Almost before the smoke of battle dies away, families start drifting back to their homes. Almost all of them find only a mass of rubble, of course, but I have not yet met one who was not sincerely grateful to see us. We know, of course, that Hitler still has a number of henchmen among the civilian population so even when they smile their greeting from ear to ear, we greet them with one finger securely on the trigger.

We've been having a good deal of rain here. With overcast skies between the showers, there is no denying that the air force has been unable to give us the amount of help that we had hoped. To maintain their precision bombings of clearly defined targets mapped out in Britain is one thing. That they can do with no visibility at all. But to follow the shifting course of a battle and be available for knocking out pill-boxes and installations which do not appear on a map; that is something else again. You will hear of much more rapid progress being made when they are able to throw the full weight of their power into the fight. We have counted heavily on them. They'll do a magnificent job. I seldom see a German plane in the air in the daytime. We have complete mastery of the skies. At night, however, they do their best to sneak through and it will no doubt be many a week before any of us enjoy the luxury of a complete night of uninterrupted sleep.

Now I must sign off. I trust you are as much at peace about the present and future as I. God is taking such wonderful care of me that I just do not want you to worry one bit. There is no limit to His wisdom and might and His confidential fellowship is with those that fear Him.

June 15, 1944

Well, apart from the war we are getting along O.K. We could use a good cook. We have no kitchens, of course. But with a little one-burner gas pressure stove we manage to heat our canned food so we have enough each day. It doesn't taste too bad, either.

I was often told how impossible it would be to have services under combat conditions. I am now almost convinced that such a decision is the convenient excuse of men who consider it a chore to have services. It may get worse later on, of course, and it may be more difficult in other units than the type I am with. But from my experience, I have had better opportunities here than ever. Men not only welcome my coming around and talking to them, but are glad to have services. I have been having two a day almost every day since my arrival and Sunday I had five. The groups must of necessity be much smaller than in garrison. No men are allowed to leave their guns more than a few feet. But I always set up my altar arrangement on the hood of my jeep, and we sing a couple of songs. After prayer I preach from ten to fifteen minutes and then while my clerk distributes V-Mail to men who need it, I invite any men who wish to partake of communion to come forward and I take care of them.

The morale of the men is very good. They have been happy at the opportunity to start writing home even though we have no idea when the letters get through. We have not yet received mail and may not for another week or more.

June 21, 1944 - Services in the Field, France

Yesterday, in spite of unsettled weather, we did have two services. I'm going to write a bit about them for Faith & Fellowship. They were both somewhat interrupted by planes strafing the area from just above the trees. Only one lad was hit and he will live. I know for certain of two of the planes being brought down. We always are sure when we line up for a service that we have good camouflage for the men and that fox-holes are close by. As soon as we spot the planes we just dive into the holes and wait until they are past, then we come out and start in again where we left off. It certainly makes for variety in the service, I can assure you. But I repeat what I have said before; it is almost unbelievable how accustomed one gets to it. I cannot sense that it affects my nerves one bit or even quickens my heart-beat. It is really something to thank God for. And I do. It would be demoralizing to the troops and a reflection on the Gospel of Christ if I were to show anxiety, not to mention fear. Not all are constituted so fortunately. It is no reflection on them. You simply have it or you haven't.

Now I take off for the hospital to see the boy who was shot at our service yesterday. I visited him last night but they had him under ether then and were operating. We cannot keep up with all the casualties but when they are close by, we try to visit them periodically.

June 26, 1944

Yesterday was a big day. I had eight services for groups from 24 to 68 in number. I was amazed at the way my voice held out. These men are poor singers so it is quite a strain to lead the song service and drag them along. But I refuse to let them sit like bumps on a log. The service cannot possibly mean as much to them unless they take active part. So I keep booming away and then have them read the Scripture and also pray the Lord's Prayer. But they certainly enjoy hearing the Gospel. So many who make no pretense of being Christians come to tell me how much the message means to them. But I was washed out when the day was over and will not have a single service today. I want to rest. Our boss Chaplain has intimated that he may take one of my groups from me, as I have too much to do. He has another Chaplain in his office (incidentally, that is the position that was offered me some months ago) who does practically nothing. So my work may ease up a little.

Now I must end my chatting for today. I've really been able to write without much interruption today. Only once did Jerry come over to strafe us. One lad was hit pretty bad by a shell that went through his steel helmet but he was still alive when they took him to the hospital. And so it goes day by day. It is tragic to see young life snuffed out so ruthlessly. But even so, for every one that gets hit, thousands in the same area are missed. Is it not only common sense that God can and will number me among those thousands just as long as He sees that His cause and you need me? That is my confidence today, and each day. Good-bye for now.

"When life's perils o'er me hover,
He will keep.
My defenseless head He covers,
He will keep.

Underneath my Saviour's arms,
He'll support in fierce alarms,
And from ev'ry loss and harm,
He will keep."

July 3, 1944 - "And the Rains Fell, France

"Because of the rain" (Acts 28:2) might well explain many things in reference to our present situation as well as Paul's condition on the isle of Malta. The sun has never been out for more than an hour, I think, since we landed. The other day we even had a cloud-burst mixed with hail. Day and night it pours or drips so the sky is like lead above and the ground underfoot is goo. Since so much of our work depends on adequate observation for long distances, both on the ground and from the air, it is easy to understand how handicapped we have been. Living discomforts are multiplied, of course, and there is nothing that any of us can do about it except bring to our miserable conditions the best humor that we can muster. When you cannot improve your situation then try to improve your attitude toward your situation. And when you are sound in body, and your mind and soul are at peace with God and man, it is truly amazing how much you can do by conscious effort along this line.

Church services have been quite curtailed of late, but I try to make up for that by plodding around and talking to the men. Yesterday I had only three services. Some of these are held under some very unusual conditions. Last Friday I had one in a machine shed which also served as a chicken coop. The interior decorating was not of the latest Park Avenue design but in the pouring rain it did enable us to keep dry. We set up the organ between the shafts of a one-horse hay rake. My altar I set up on a manure wheel-barrow over which I had thrown a raincoat. For my pulpit I used two big chunks of wood, set end on end. The men sat on the ground or on pieces of machinery. And there we worshiped for forty-five minutes on the 136th Psalm, "God's mercy endureth forever."

Celebrating July 4th

Today is trying very hard to be an exception to the rule. We have had only a few drops of rain. So I have made use of the very unusual weather to get my clothes washed. You should have seen the French here celebrate the 4th. Our only celebration was to fire a great concentration from every gun on a target just at noon. But the French had made ropes of beautiful flowers; some were artificial but most were real, and they were draped about the doors, windows and fences.

Everywhere were placards printed in English and French "Welcome to our Liberators," "The French people are grateful," "Long live France, Long live America." I watched a whole delegation place wreaths at the American flag pole in the soldiers cemetery by the beach. In every little town the people were gathered to hear speeches in French. Along all roads, women and children handed us flowers as we drove by. Many little girls had on red, white and blue dresses. They were simply adorable. It was all very festive and did our hearts good.

July 10, 1944

We have now put in quite a few days and nights of firing. Except for the constant rain, I have not suffered too much. I get along O.K. on our canned food it seems.

We are so much more fortunate than many of the other troops. Being completely motorized, we have gas for heating water and cooking coffee. Also we are able to haul enough water both to drink and wash. Also, you realize that our big guns have a tremendous range so we can be some distance from our front line targets. We can, therefore, move around much more freely than the infantry, for instance, who must plod along on foot and for whom every tree and building is a potential sniper's hideout. Of course, the German guns reach us just as well as ours reach them, and we get to fight out some lively duels at frequent intervals. The most irritating thing about it is that most of it is done during the night, the early morning or late evening. Most of the danger from planes, on the other hand, is during the day. Another factor that counts against us, naturally, is the size of the projectiles. Whereas an infantryman's rifle shot kills one man, a cannon shell or rocket may get a couple of dozen.

In the light of this, it is simply remarkable how few casualties we have had. Miraculous escapes have been so many that we lose count. But I seldom have a service but what I have occasion to render special thanks to God for His wondrous protection over the men of that unit since last we met. Just yesterday in one of my groups, four immense shells had lit just the night before. Two of the boys' slit trenches were only 25 feet apart. They had dived into these when some shells began to drop close. Then one lit half-way between the two, almost suffocating them with dirt in their trenches but neither of them got a scratch. When that one lit, another boy left his tent where he had been sleeping and slid into his trench. He had no sooner hit the bottom than a shell tore his pup-tent and bedding-roll to ribbons. I saw them afterward. He had not gotten a scratch. In the afternoon yesterday a rocket lit near one of our vehicles. Shelling had been going on for some time and most of the lads had been in their trenches. But in a lull in the firing, a lad had left his trench to go and cook a cup of coffee under a nearby tree. One of the rockets lit smack in the bottom of the trench he had just vacated and blasted dirt for fifty feet around. Well you just can't go on day after day experiencing this sort of thing without believing in a miracle-working God and while many of the fellows are inclined to ascribe it all to their good luck, I do not miss any opportunities to remind them of God's daily care for us, as unworthy as we are. I repeatedly remind them that our light casualties are to a large extent the result of the prayers and tears of loved ones at home. And they take it, too.

July 17, 1944 - CASUALTIES, France

I have not been having a great number of services lately. Men cannot well be spared from their guns. Neither is it safe to gather any group of them in one place. So I go about speaking to them as individuals or at each gun and pray with them. Especially when there is a good deal of action, they appreciate so much to see the Chaplain going among them. They are pretty much just boys then, and they need the steadying hand of someone who knows God and has seen a bit more of life than they have. The officers are not the least grateful for my presence. Not having faith in God themselves, they lack what these men need. Just one case will suffice.

Saturday I was calling on one of my units to inquire if they thought it possible to get the men together for a service on Sunday morning. Both the first Sargent and the C.O. agreed that this would be very welcome and O.K. since it seemed they were in an especially well-protected area. We had no sooner spoken than we had to hit the dirt on our faces as a shell came screaming through the air. It hit about 50 feet away and showered us with twigs, dirt and rocks. As the noise of the explosion faded, one of the lads began yelling, "Help, help, I'm hit!" I jumped over a hedge and found fellows standing around and no one able to move. I found the foxhole where the boy was and with some severity ordered two lads to give me a hand in pulling him out and sent another off to get a first-aid man and the ambulance. The lad had a brutal hole in his back. He could not live. While others bandaged him, I knelt beside him and prayed. He had died before we had gotten him into the ambulance. Another sacrifice to the god of war.

After it was all over, I found the C.O. Where he had been in the meantime I do not know. But he said, "Chaplain, I'm mighty glad you were here to take charge of things." So I told him that I would spend the rest of the afternoon among his men. The enemy had found the range of this unit and were therefore pouring a good deal of shells about. So I spent about half of my time ducking in and out of fox-holes. But I guess the presence of a Chaplain has never meant more than to those men that day.

It was a rough day for our units. Quite a number died and I was busy until midnight visiting others in field hospitals. Our own guns as well as those of the enemy kept up a terrific barrage all night so we were not in the best humor for Sunday. However, by today it has let up somewhat. I slept well last night. The sun has been shining today so our air force is out in large numbers. That prevents the enemy from sneaking with their planes in and out among the clouds to observe our positions and dropping fire on us.

Most of my religious magazines as well as Readers Digest have now caught up with me. It is an intellectual as well as a spiritual tonic to get these papers. Today, then, in a battle-scarred country, I've been reading about spring, art, poetry, theology, church unity, post-war planning and biography.

July 20, 1944 - Misery and Ruins; Normandy, France

Rain. Rain. And more rain. Day and night. Night and day. Mud bogging down the vehicles. Your clothes soaked and muddy with nothing to change to. No place to find shelter from the constant downpour except to sit doubled over in your pup-tent. It's too dark in there to read, and writing is out of the question. So you lie under the blanket in your wet clothes hoping that body heat will dry out most of it or at least warm up the wet that clings to you from head to foot. Your slit trench is a half-filled bath-tub of muddy water which you can only hope you'll not have to dive into.

This part of the country is made up of small ghost towns and farm houses. All buildings have been blasted to rubble. The people have fled leaving furniture, livestock and pets. Stray cattle roam here and there, bellowing in misery for not having been milked for days. Less fortunate ones lie injured or hobble about with festering shell wounds and broken bones. Dogs go smelling about buildings which once was home. One home where I peeked in at the open door today showed a table set for a meal with the chairs placed about it. The family had evidently been assembled as the shelling started, and they fled for their lives. It may have been our shells or that of the enemy. No one knows.

You ask, is there no alleviation of all this wretchedness and discomfort? Yes, fortunately, it is not all black. In the first place God has blessed me with a rugged constitution that gets a thrill out of splashing around in water and mud. I've walked miles in it today with the water on my face and in my boots. I actually feel good enough so I can sing as I go about among the men. Of course, there is no chance to have services, but there is much in a Christian spirit of charity and cheerfulness that counts apart from preaching. Secondly, my bed was quite dry when I turned in last night. I lay there and thanked God for that for some time. Then I always think as I see the misery about me here, that my loved ones are being spared all this and I am grateful. It is easy to endure knowing that you are all safe and happy.

Now, though the sky is still heavily overcast, it has not rained for an hour and I'm perched here on the tongue of my trailer with this [typewriter] machine on my knees and just hoping I'll be able to finish this before it starts to pour again.

From all my hiking, I'm spattered with mud to my hips. Trousers and boots would be able to stand alone and I'll not be able to bend my knees if this stuff ever dries. But there seems to be no immediate danger of that.

[Bronze Star Citation period begins August 1, 1944]

August 9, 1944 - Serving the Wounded, France

For the present I have attached myself to a field hospital which receives our battle casualties. After the last engagement I told my C.O. that I felt that I could serve more needy men here than traveling with a firing unit. You see, while we are forging ahead I could not get from one unit to another. This meant that I could only serve the men with whom I happened to be traveling. That might be about two hundred men. Of these, perhaps there would be ten to twenty casualties in a ten-day push. As for the rest of the men, they had no Chaplain then whatsoever until the engagement was over and we were sent into a rear area to re-equip and rest.

On the other hand at the hospital, there was no Chaplain. There might be two or three hundred casualties passing through each day. They are kept just long enough here to get emergency treatment and then sent some forty miles to the rear to an evacuation hospital where needed surgery is performed and then they are sent to England if they are not able to return to duty in about ten days.

My C.O. agreed that a man was certainly needed here and simply said, "Padre, I have told you that you are your own boss in the combat zone. You go wherever you believe you can do the most good. Just let me know occasionally where you are. I trust you to do your job without my supervision." So I have been here for about a week. I have some eighteen doctors and one hundred enlisted men. We have no women nurses in these forward hospitals.

So here both the dead and wounded are brought in all hours of the day and night. The dead must get to collecting points where they are prepared for burial. Whenever possible, I talk and pray with the wounded. Many, of course, were in such pain when picked up that they were immediately doped with morphine and are unable to grasp much. But many are delighted to see a Chaplain and the way they look at you and often grasp your hand makes you want to weep for them in their helplessness.

I have seen many, many sights which I can only hope and pray will not be imprinted too indelibly on the memory. The human body is no match for jagged steel and hot lead which travels faster than sound. Here we come to grips with war without the bands and brass buttons. Here it is all blood, sweat, dirt, shattered limbs and shattered minds.

I have had some wretched jobs the last few days. Last night I drove in an ambulance eighty miles with two of our pilots. One was so horribly disfigured that had I not seen his tags I would never have known it was he. Besides two broken knees, three broken ribs, a skull fracture, his face and hands were mashed to a pulp. Yet he regained consciousness occasionally and I was able to quiet him by telling him I'd stay right with him and see that he was well taken care of and that he had only to relax and sleep. He'd then quit his delirious struggles and say like a little child, "O.K., Chappy, you take care of everything."

I mentioned earlier in this letter of the conversation I had with my C.O. I had no intimation then that it would be the last time I was to speak with him. Two days later I went over to my headquarters and was told he had not been heard from since the day before. They said four tanks had been knocked out several miles down the road and they feared he was in one of them as he had gone up to see what was holding up the advance. But no one had investigated as the tanks had exploded and then burned. They had found his helmet some yards away so supposed he was in it. I understood at once that it was demoralizing to the men to let this uncertainty continue so I asked the C.O. for permission to take the C.O.'s orderly (who has been driving and taking care of everything he owns for two years) and dig through the remains in the tank to see if we could find anything. I need not try to picture the task I had of working inside this tank on a hot afternoon rooting among bits of twisted steel and pieces of bodies. I could not find another that could stomach the job to help me so I worked alone for five hours. I finally had to get a tank wrecker to pull the tank away so I could dig through all the charred remains but I was able to find what was left of four men and definitely identify three of them. I found six articles of personal equipment which my C.O. had on his person so I know he is gone. Three weeks ago he stood under a tree with his men and received Communion and asked me for a Bible. He leaves a wife and two sons.

I started this letter by saying I'm camped tonight in a lovely meadow. A short distance away is a little oat field which has been harvested today. That was a sight worth seeing. They used an ordinary mower except that behind the sickle-bar was a cradle. Two men operated the thing. One sat directly above the wheel close to the standing grain and with a long-handled rake, pulled the grain back into the cradle until this was full and he then tripped it, leaving a pile the size of a bundle. Then come all the members of the family (augmented, apparently, by one or two other families) including old ladies, girls and boys, of every age and size. These arrange themselves around the field and tie the bundles with grain and pull them out of the way of the machine before it comes around the next time. The fields are not more than an acre or two in size so it looks more like they are playing at farming than the real thing. They shock the bundles in round shocks and then set one upside-down on top to keep out the rain. If my films come, I hope to get some pictures of some harvesting scenes. It is unbelievable that people can be so primitive in our day.

You can gather from this peaceful agricultural scene that war has not hit this country too hard. That is true. Our advance through this section has been so rapid that there has been little destruction of life or property right here. Strategic cities, industries and railroads have been blasted to the skies, of course, but I've passed through many a small town lately where shops and bakeries are operating and the women sit out front knitting. The Germans have gotten the worst of it so many times meeting us on equal terms that they no longer try to defend every foot of soil. They hold important ridges, crossroads and towns with fanatic tenacity but when we have blasted them there, we may go on from there almost without interference until we approach the next strong-point. The other day, we advanced forty miles into this area. Then we may fight several days to gain one hundred yards.

Well, now that's enough on the war situation for this time.

I've been looking forward to berry time here. You've heard all about these hedgerows over here that divide up the land into about five hundred foot squares. In addition to the bushes and trees which grow in each of these, they are all a-tangle with blackberry bushes. So far the only dividend these vines have paid is that they have practically torn our skin to ribbons as we dig our slit trenches along the ditches. Today, however, I found several luscious berries.

August 14, 1944 - France

No assignment in this war has served as well as the present one to make me willing to struggle on foreign soil. Since I last wrote, we have had some terrific bombings. The center of one of these a few nights ago was a lovely little town about a mile from our hospital. Planes swooped over our heads again and again for the bombing run. As far as we can understand, they thought that we had set up our headquarters in this town which up to that time was almost entirely unharmed. But on this night they went through a veritable nightmare of horror. Not only were all our ambulances bringing in one load of soldier casualties after the other, but after midnight they started bringing in loads of civilians. I pray God we may not have to live through such a night of misery again soon. Babies not more than a year, tousled-haired boys and girls, men and women up to seventy and eighty, these had been found under debris, covered with dust and dirt. Should I tell you of just one concrete case? If you'd rather not hear, just skip this next paragraph.

About 1:00 a.m. a grandmother brought in a baby girl. The old lady was bare-footed, her hair filled with dirt hanging about her face. The baby she carried in her feeble arms was crying weakly. We removed the tattered quilt as we set the dazed old lady over to one side and gave her a cup of coffee. Uncovering the child's head, we saw that both eyes were blackened and swollen shut and bits of flesh had been torn away on various parts of the face. Turning the head gently to one side, we found a shrapnel wound right through the base of the skull, behind the ear. That looked bad. But having carefully washed and disinfected these injuries, we undressed her further to find her left forearm was broken. This we dressed with splints and bandaged. That should be enough wreckage for one body, but as we removed the rest of her rags, we found her right leg was laying grotesquely across the other, the bone between hip and knee completely severed and muscles and ligaments chewed and torn by jagged shrapnel. How she had survived until we had cared for her, I cannot imagine. We saw no hope of her survival and I offered a prayer there for her soul, committing it to the care of Him who said, "Let the little children come unto me and forbid them not, for of such is the kingdom of heaven." Then we turned to the grandmother and told her that the child would be evacuated to a hospital further to the rear and that she could go along in the ambulance. She thanked us but said she could not, as she had left four other little children alone and must return to them. Before daylight she had brought in two others, wounded and suffering. Now the sequel to this story is that just yesterday one of our doctors visited that rear area hospital and that poor little baby is still alive and appears to be gaining. This sulfa and penicillin does wonders.

It is against a dark background that little tokens of love, thoughtfulness and cooperation shine the brightest. So here is a bit from my experience with my men. Last Saturday night Ramsey says, "Chaplain, do you know the boys are planning to put up a tent for your service in the morning?" I had not heard of it. But sure enough, directly after breakfast, these GI's get together without an officer to order or direct them, and start raising an immense ward tent. I went over and said, "Fellows, surely you're not going to all this work just for my service?" They said, "Why not, Chaplain. It's the biggest thing that happens to us here all week." Well, you just can't show your appreciation properly for that kind of spirit. For an hour they sweat and worked in the sun just so we could have it a bit church-like for our services.

The biggest news for us and the world over the radio today has been the landings of allied forces in southern France. That is a move we've been awaiting for a month. We have known for a long time of fully equipped and trained French troops in Algeria awaiting the word to strike. They have quite a force and supported as they are in this landing by American and British troops and aided by the fact that the Germans do not seem to have nearly the strength there that they had in Normandy, we should see some mighty rapid advancement made there in the next few days as they plow northward to join us.

I am enclosing the copy which revealed for the first time the presence of our outfit over here. You will note that they had achieved something of a reputation as fighters already. They have certainly done their share in this invasion.

I continue in the best of health. You will be glad to hear that we are having better food here than I have ever had in this country. Hospitals generally feed a bit better as they are able to take their field kitchens with them and thus prepare food properly. (However, do not jump to the conclusion from this statement that there was anything the matter with the food I was preparing). We even have a doctor who can test beef so we have been authorized to buy a steer. You'd think these folks would be glad to make a donation like that but they let us pay. So we take up a collection from all the men, butcher the thing and live like kings for a couple of days. We paid forty dollars for the steer and have been paying 60¢ a dozen for eggs. The men do not object, of course, as they have no earthly use for their money here. There's not a chance to spend it. It is reported that they are now saving 90 per cent of their wages.

August 23, 1944 - On the way to Paris

Tonight's radio brings us the thrilling news of the liberation of Paris. The French are hilarious, of course. No victory could mean more to them. We are glad it was done as it was. Had the French not taken it from within the city itself, it is entirely possible the Germans would have fortified it and we would have had to bomb and shell them out. This would have cost thousands of lives both civilian and military, besides the untold destruction of homes and means of livelihood.

The broadcast reached us just as we had pulled into the area which will probably be our home for at least part of the night. We are spending three-fourths of our time on the road these days and each mile is bringing us closer to our final objectives. The hours of travel, however, do not indicate the distance traveled as measured in peacetime travel. I think almost every road in France, including dirt side roads and trails, are black with the movement of troops, weapons and equipment. Where these cross, there are bound to be long delays. But none of us feel like complaining. The more stuff the better. Just keep it rolling in

We hardly have time to eat or sleep. Pack and unpack. Sometimes several times a day. But again, no complaints -- because each move brings the end nearer. After several days of beautiful weather, it now seems we're in for some rain. In fact, this letter is getting wet right now so I'll have to sign off to continue later if it lets up.

August 25. Well, it got to be quite some time before I had a chance to continue this letter. As I stated, we had just pulled into a bivouac for the night. It was a rather pleasant place where I had even found a patch of grass on which to lay my blankets. But as the rain started pouring, they called us to supper and a half-hour later we were ordered to be on the road again. In a drenching rain we rode for miles in inky blackness. Wrecked German vehicles jutting out into the highways everywhere makes such driving particularly hazardous and drivers' nerves and tempers wear pretty thin. About midnight they pulled us off the road into a barley field. We immediately set to work putting up the ward and surgery tents. That, too, is some job with the soaked canvas as heavy as lead and trying to keep track of everything (pegs, ropes and poles) in the darkness.

The job was only well begun when the drone of planes were heard overhead. Jerries. The whole area was soon as bright as Times Square as they dropped showers of flares to light up their targets. By their light, I dug like a gopher to get some kind of a foxhole. By the time it was four inches deep and several inches too short, they were back and the bombs started dropping.

As you may have gathered, I'm still traveling with our aid station. We have no evidence that they will purposely bomb a hospital, but we all recognize that it is not always easy to distinguish this as such until the damage is done. Besides, as we are getting closer to our goal, it is only reasonable to suppose that they become more and more desperate and may resort to anything. So we prepare for the worst.

We spent a wretched hour with our faces in the dirt as one plane after the other roared in and unloaded their cargo of death on a nearby road where one of our convoys was passing.

I have learned since that several were killed, including the captain who first welcomed me into this outfit and has ever since been my staunch friend.

The rain which began that evening kept up all night and all the next day. The old barley field became a quagmire. Everything we have is again caked with mud and thoroughly wet. But this, too, will pass.

Enemy Patients

Patients that have come in during the last 36 hours have been mostly enemy. Many of these have been ready to surrender just as fast as our troops can get to them to take the men. There are, however, still many tough pockets where they have dug themselves in and where fanatic Nazis will fight as long as they can pull a trigger. Even as they lay dying, they'll maintain that Germany will win. We have captured many Russians, Poles, Latvians, etc. These have been largely slaves from occupied countries who at the point of a gun have been required to do all the manual labor for the Germans while Nazis were serving in the army. Many of these are pathetic. Last night they brought in a Russian lad who said he was 17 but which I question was no more than 15. He had been wounded in the leg and had cried all the way to the hospital for fear of what we would do to him (after listening to German lies of American atrocities for a couple of years). We happened to have a lad who could speak to him in Russian. In a half hour we had him treated, fed him a hot meal, and with face beaming like a child, he had fallen to sleep on a cot (which incidentally, none of us are allowed to use.)

Since I wrote the first paragraphs, word has reached us of Rumania's capitulation. That is great. Of course, it may not mean more than the capitulation of Italy where we have still had a tough job routing the Germans and German sympathizers. It does, however, show that many of Hitler's staunch friends, who with him launched the campaign for world dominion, are losing faith, one by one, in him and his program and are getting out while they yet can save something.

Our own advance continues with breath-taking speed. And as it advances, it grows in power. New units join the drive daily. Casualties are more than replaced at once with well-trained men. Vehicles either get excellent repair at once or are replaced by the endless convoys of ships unloading at the docks.

[Bronze Star Citation period ends August 31, 1944]

September 8, 1944 [letter to daughter, age 11]

My darling daughter,

"In all thy ways acknowledge him (Jesus) and he shall direct thy paths."

That simply means that if you, everywhere you go, will let it be known that you love Jesus, He will always keep you safely from harm and from sin and will use your life to glorify His Name. It has made me very happy to hear both through your own letters and through mother's that you are telling others of His goodness. God bless and keep you and all of us busy winning souls until Jesus comes.

Well, Daddy is covering a lot of country these days. The Germans have been on the run for two weeks now and it keeps us on the go to keep up. We would be much further than we are, except that we must not run ahead of our gas supply which now has to be hauled by trucks a long way. They haul night and day. At night they must drive very slowly because the road has been bombed out to leave great holes and since we cannot use any lights, you have to be careful. Sometimes the drivers do not get to sleep for several days. They keep awake by drinking black coffee and always remembering that thousands of lives depend on their convoy getting through.

The weather has been bad for two weeks. On our last jump we traveled seventy-five miles in one day. All forenoon we drove on cross-country dirt roads which were rough and where the dust was so thick you could hardly see the truck ahead. By afternoon it started to rain and kept pouring down. We must keep our windshield down on our jeep and of course we do not have the top up, so we are thoroughly soaked before long. We finally reached the place we are to camp at midnight. It is in the middle of a grain field again where the wheels and your boots, too, sink into the mud. There, in the pasting rain we unroll our blankets in the mud and crawl in to get what sleep we can before daylight when the whistle blows and we must be on the road again. It is quite cold here, too, now.

You would get a great thrill out of seeing how happy the people are that we have come. I do not think they are getting any work done either on the farms or in the cities. Everyone seems to be out beside the road waving a greeting. They stand by the hour as our long columns pass by. Many, many cry for joy. Some know a few words of English and shout, "Welcome!" *"Vive la Amerique!"* "Thank you!" When the column stops, as it does many times a day, they crowd around you to shake your hand. The mothers hold up their babies to kiss you on both cheeks (of course, they then expect you to give them some candy or rations). In a little town two days ago we stopped for a while. A young woman who could speak a few English words told us that the Germans had been there for four years. Several days before we came they had not been allowed to leave their houses for three days or they would be shot. That was because their men had refused to work for nothing and a little food in the coal mines. She told of how a little girl ten years old had been shot because she had not greeted a German officer. One day someone had killed a German soldier so they gathered up twenty of the townspeople and shot them. The young lady said as we left, and the tears of thankfulness streamed down her cheeks, "And now the Americans have come and we are all so thankful." How glad I am that my little girl does not have to live in a constant terror of cruel guns. And I'm glad, too, that I can have a little share in making these people free again.

The people along the road stand with baskets of fruit which they throw at our vehicles as we pass. Most of the apples are really too green to eat, but they have nothing more to give. Others throw pears and then they have the biggest blue plums I have ever seen. They are delicious and I've been eating dozens of them. We buy some potatoes and eggs too.

September 11, 1944 – Somewhere in Belgium

Greetings from the land of wooden shoes, large white, starched bonnets and great, lazy windmills. We are now permitted to say we have entered this story-book country. It is as picturesque as a fairyland. Never have we met people as friendly and as wildly enthusiastic about our coming.

We are now parked in a little pasture. Two fine Belgian yearling colts come sniffing around our tents at night. In the afternoon and evening the civilians come in by the dozens bringing great clothes baskets of tomatoes, plums, apples, pears, melons, and buckets of milk. Eggs, butter and coarse bread baked in a chimney oven are available just for the asking. They never cease to wonder that the American Army lives and eats in the field. When the Germans moved in on them, they took possession of their houses, and the people themselves had to move into the barn if they wanted to stay. All the while the army was here, they butchered anything they wanted. Of course, they never paid a cent for anything. If and when we use their produce, we insist on paying or giving in exchange whatever we have that they can use. As for food, they have enough in the country, except for chocolate. They ask us so winsomely if we have any "shokolat." Then the women have no soap and the men have no cigarettes. These items most of the soldiers have in abundance so everyone is happy.

The chief farm products are potatoes and sugar beets. Just now the whole family is out digging the potatoes, row after row, with pitchforks. Beet refineries are getting their machinery in condition and steam in their boilers to process a bumper crop.

So far, the dairy herds which I have seen are not large. The farmers sell whole milk to co-operative creameries where the world-famous cheeses and butter are prepared.

A plebiscite would certainly never swing this country for Hitler and his gang. As we travel further inland, we all notice the intense hatred and vengeance which the populace feels toward Nazism. Refined women and cultured men line the sidewalks of towns, wave their arms in hilarious greeting to our columns and then hiss out the name of Hitler and yell out, "Hitler kapot" (Hitler is through) "De Bosch" – and then they draw the edge of their hand across their throat in a meaning only too apparent. Everywhere they want to know how many more days it will be before the war is over. At least once it has already been broadcast over their radio that Germany had capitulated and the wild enthusiasm that day made it almost impossible for our convoys to move on the roads.

The morale of the troops being what it is, the work of the Chaplain becomes a pleasure. Men are cheerful, cooperative and face their problems and inconveniences with a hopefulness that is contagious. Our casualties for quite some time have been unbelievably light. By far the largest number of patients passing through our field hospitals are German. Those of our men who are wounded have almost invariably as their greatest concern that they will be taken out of the rest of the fight and returned to a hospital in England.

Their next greatest concern is that their parents will be worried about them when they hear. My prayers with them always must include petitions to God that loved ones may not be unduly anxious. Could the folks at home see the prompt and expert care, the tender consideration given all these lads by the doctors and male nurses, they would be much relieved and thank God.

As to religious services, I am glad to say that I get every cooperation from both officers and men in holding services whenever the tactical situation permits. While we are actually firing it is, of course, impossible to gather the men for public services. We then go from one gun to another offering such words of counsel and cheer as God may inspire us to speak, and frequently there is a lull where all of us at a particular gun can bow our heads for a brief word of prayer and a verse from God's Word.

But as soon as an engagement is over and we pull out of firing positions to do maintenance on guns and vehicles, as well as bring up supplies and replacements of men, the men begin looking for a chance to attend services. I try to get to each unit for a service once a week, but that is not always possible. I have held as many as eight services a day and quite often we have had services every day of the week. The attendance as well as the response of the men would gladden the hearts of all true pastors who are burdened for the souls of men. As I have said so many times before, I could not have asked God to have given me a more blessed ministry in which to invest my energy and time these years. May God keep us busy in the King's business that each day may be fully invested to the glory of God and the salvation of our fellowmen.

I have had some very fine services over this weekend. One of my Battalions was not committed to action so they had plenty of time to assemble and they really made use of it. I had five services Sunday and two on Monday. For each one we set up our altar and got out the organ. I managed to have services the last day we were in France just as I had them the first day we were there. I was glad for that.

The Library of Louvain

Yesterday, in looking for some units, I managed to get in a sightseeing trip I'll never forget. I visited the city of Louvain (look it up on the map). There is a great university there, but to us it is especially interesting as the world-renowned library which was erected and maintained by the colleges of America and the Rockefeller Foundation and presented as a gift of the American people to Belgium after the last war. One of the Hitlerites' worst atrocities was committed here as they set fire to the building in the early stages of the war. It was of no military significance whatsoever, so it was an act of pure barbarism. Though tons of books and manuscripts had been removed to the U.S.A. for safe-keeping, still one million volumes were destroyed by the flames which left this majestic building which covers an entire square block and rises above the city skyline to about eighteen stories, a shell in which the walls remained. It made you sick to go from one floor to the other of debris covered casements, where columns and colonades were still covered with black soot and the marks of countless book racks could still be seen along the wall.

I counted myself very fortunate in that the old custodian, learning that I was a clergyman, brought out the only album of pictures of the place in all its original beauty and presented them to me.

September 20, 1944 – Belgium

I had a grand sleep last night. About nine hours of it. There was very little firing as the fog was so thick they could not well observe targets. So I feel grand today. Sleep is a wonderful restorer.

The farms about here are in grand shape. Almost all the crops are harvested except the fruit which is ripening rapidly. The dairy herds have been pretty badly depleted by the Jerries, but what is left looks good and provides adequate dairy products for home use. You see, this country before the war supplied immense amounts to England. So they are the ones who are suffering now rather than these people. The war passed by these folks so quickly that most of their homes are intact and there have been few civilian casualties. Most people of the middle class are better dressed than folks were in England and have better food. Their greatest demand is for cigarettes and chocolate, both of which I think they can well do without.

Most of them are so hilariously enthusiastic about our coming that they are a nuisance. However, there are many exceptions. There have been large numbers of folks here who married men of the German army. Many found it profitable to do business with them and many others have always been Nazis just as we have them in America. We must, therefore, be on our guard and not trust them. They may be sincere but it is quite probable that the most enthusiastic are working for Hitler and just await a chance to get information or stab you in the back. It is a problem to teach these trusting Americans to be suspicious. So we sometimes have tragedies that make you sick.

September 27, 1944

BRONZE STAR MEDAL CITATION

HEADQUARTERS 2nd ARMORED DIVISION
Office of the Division Commander
APO 252

200.6 Walstad, Clarence E.

SUBJECT: Award of Bronze Star Medal

TO   : Captain Clarence E. Walstad, 0-488466,
Corps of Chaplains, United States Army

Under the provisions of Army Regulation 600-45, as amended, you are awarded a Bronze Star Medal for meritorious service by Section IV, General Order Number 45, this headquarters, dated 27 September 1944, as set forth in the following:

CITATION

Captain Clarence E. Walstad, 0-488466, Corps of Chaplains, Headquarters Division Artillery, 2d Armored Division, United States Army. For meritorious service from 1 August 1944 to 31 August 1944, in France, in connection with military operations against the enemy. During the period 1 August to 31 August 1944, Chaplain Walstad stationed himself with Company C, 48th Armored Medical Battalion, where he rendered invaluable service to the sick and wounded passing through that station. Chaplain Walstad, through untiring effort, also performed church services for the five artillery battalions of this command during the same period, and made himself readily available to all artillery personnel for consultations on religious matters. The unselfish and unceasing efforts of Chaplain Walstad were a continuous inspiration to the members of the Division Artillery Command and to all those with whom he made contact, and are a distinct credit to himself and to the service. Entered military service from New York.

115

/s/ E. N. Harmon

E. N. HARMON,
Major General, U. S. Army,
Commanding

September 28, 1944 - A Baptist Parsonage Somewhere in Holland

You could never guess where I am at this moment. I am sitting in a cushioned chair, with an electric heater at my side, my typewriter on a table and surrounded by shelves of books on every side. How come all this luxury?

Well, we have been bivouacked on the outskirts of a fair-sized town for a few days. No civilians are allowed to enter the camp as we are surrounded by too many German collaborators, but three young women came to the gate to invite the men to come to a church in the town where the ladies wished to serve them a supper. It turns out that the invitation comes from a Baptist Church. Well, I did not see the young ladies; we were not allowed to leave the camp to accept the invitation but it did not take me long to begin to make inquiries about this church and its pastor. Yesterday I found him and spent a most blessed hour with him. Both he and his wife get along very well with English. They have a lovely, though simply furnished home. The library has fully 100 English theological books. The lady offered to do my washing and I was invited to come here any day and every day I could to read, write or take a nap. Who am I to deny myself such a privilege?

Since I was here yesterday, they have received word that some five Christian people from a town a few miles away have had their house bombed to the ground. They have sent word to the preacher that they have no place to go so may they come here. They were told they might sleep here, but that there was no food to eat. (I saw what the family had for dinner today. The whole menu consisted of potatoes, nothing more.) Well, I decided that called for some good Samaritan work, so went to my outfit and cleaned out the kitchen of odds and ends of canned foods and crackers that the men would not eat, and came back with two large boxes of provisions. Their gratitude has really been pathetic. Next to feeding the soul that hungers, with the everlasting Gospel, there is nothing that gives so much joy as to help fill half-starved bodies.

So, I now have the run of the house. Outside the sky is leaden gray. But here I sit like a king. God is indeed good.

You will no doubt wonder if it is possible that it rains as much as I indicate in my letters. The natives here say that throughout the year it rains twenty days each month and that this is the real rainy season. This we can well believe. We have not seen the sun for more than an hour or two for many days. If we do not develop webbed feet it will be a miracle.

October 2, 1944 - In Holland

Another Sunday has passed. The situation did not enable me to do a great deal for my troops. So in the morning I had the privilege of attending a Dutch Reformed Church. The place was very simple and the service anything but elaborate. But it was filled with reverent people and I was pleased to find that I could understand much of what was said because of the similarity of this language to Norwegian. An interesting feature of their songbook is that they have all the Psalms set to music and the words written in meter - like the Scotch.

They have only one service a week and are speechless to hear of our American church program. (More and more, I too, am convinced that we are "overchurched.") So I asked and received permission to conduct our service there in the evening instead of having it out in the muddy field. We set up our altar and field organ (at their request) and permitted their people to attend. There must have been about 100 civilians. I preached a usual army sermon which must be both evangelical and interesting. The men had a good laugh a couple of times at stories I told. I was informed afterwards that it was the first time they had ever laughed in that church. I tried to apologize for having abused my privilege as a guest if I had offended anyone, but was assured that it was all perfectly O.K. and that the people had enjoyed it. Afterward I was invited to the pastor's home where a dozen invited guests were gathered and where they fired questions at me for two hours about American church and state. They all spoke quite fluent English so it was most enjoyable.

And then I suppose that the next item of interest is that I have sent off a box to you which I expect I shall designate a Christmas Box. However, there is nothing especially Christmasy about it except the love that inspired each article and which I sent with it on its journey. But, as you perhaps realize, we have no "gift wrapping department" here in the fox-holes. The container is a ration box. The paper which I pieced together is from bandage wrappings. There was no string to tie up each article. But it is the best I could do. I now only hope it reaches you safely and in time for the holidays.

Now I must conclude by giving you another of the many miracles which God is performing each day to preserve us alive and to remind us that since He is caring for us, we need have no anxieties about our safety. Believe it or not, I had a bed to sleep in last night. It was wonderful and I thanked God until I went to sleep for the joyous luxury of lying between sheets. I regretted that I no longer carried pajamas with me or I'd have had them on to make it complete. At any rate, I was sleeping like a log at 2:00 a.m. when I was awakened by a terrific blast and a shower of heavy objects on the roof. It was a bomb, of course. I was just getting into some clothes when the man of the house came in to take me to the shelter in the basement before the next blast should come. There were no others so I went out in the moonlight to see the damage. About 20 feet from the front door, a large bomb had landed right in the middle of the paved street. These bombs are set so that they are supposed to go off as soon as they hit and thus throw their deadly steel in a thousand directions causing all the damage possible. This one had instead buried itself ten feet or more in the road before it exploded. Thus the steel and most of the blast was absorbed by the roadway. Dirt had been thrown over an area of a whole block and some had hurled through an open window and covered the bed where the people of the house slept. But not one soul had even been injured all because God ordained that this bomb should go off a second or two late. In a half hour I was sound asleep again. Are not the ways of God wonderful? How can we sin against Him by failing to trust Him every moment? We'll rest in Him, will we not, and let each day demonstrate that "no man putting his trust in the Lord has ever been put to shame."

Holland and its People

There are stores here, too. The windows show quite modern styles along the lines of American design. But inflation has so skyrocketed prices that only the wealthy can buy. A package of cigarettes is worth $3 and folks would much rather accept them than money. Coffee (by the way, in the box I sent, there is a blue envelope containing coffee of the kind the Germans sold here for $60 a pound. It is roasted barley, I think, and to my palate is hardly drinkable) cannot be bought but there is some tea. Almost all dairy cattle were taken by the Germans so butter is practically non-existent. The gardens do very well so they have plenty of greens now and the good harvest on their small farms will give them flour and feed this winter.

Most of the homes here are beautiful. They seem to be mostly of modern design in the villages and cities. They have overstuffed furniture, large windows, beautiful flowers and house-plants but few lawns. Their dishes and silverware are beautiful. Almost all families have maids. In the better homes they pay them $10 a week. Many homes have a piano of some sort and quite a number of the men play the violin. All you have heard about the cleanliness of Hollanders is true. I have actually seen women with mop and scrub bucket out washing the cobblestones of the highway. Their homes and linen are a delight with their cleanliness, and even though shoes may be patched and collars frayed from wear after years of German occupation, they are always clean. They look much like Norwegians. Most of them are fair with blue eyes and of medium height. The women are inclined to be stout with a sturdy stockiness which is not soft fat.

Besides the preacher, I have visited in the home of a mining engineer whose wife has a M.A. degree in Botany. I spent a wonderful evening in the home of the leading doctor in town. He is not a Christian and told me so but he nevertheless has urged me to visit his wife's best friend who just recently lost her husband and was left with three little children. He said, "I believe your cheerful assurance and faith would do her more good than any prescription I could offer." I must try to go tomorrow.

WE ENTER GERMANY: Fighting in the Siegfried Line

Yes, the Siegfried Line has been broken in several places. In a number of places we have found that they had not even had time to get guns or men put into the massive concrete forts which we call "pill-boxes." From some others, the Jerries have come out with their hands in the air before a shot has been fired. But we cannot fool ourselves. Most of the line is offering the toughest resistance we have had. Progress will be slow and the price terrific. It is to be hoped that as we break through at one place after the other, that they will see the futility of trying to hold and will withdraw to the Rhine. As I have traveled from one unit to the other up there at the front today, it has certainly impressed me as uninviting country. The civilians are anxious to show how glad they are that we have come. But we are not being fooled. Many of them would slit our throats if we turned our backs. Had they been so ready to welcome us, they could easily have found ways of aiding our patrols with valuable information earlier in the fight.

October 9, 1944 - Holland

I have come a long way over this continent of Europe since I last wrote. Much of it has been surprisingly easy going as the Germans do not have the men, equipment or natural defense positions to try holding each mile. But they make desperate stands when they do dig in. For a number of days now we have been slugging it out here. The constant rains keep us fairly miserable. The Jerries have concentrated vast amounts of artillery here as we also have. The result is such fireworks day and night as you have never seen. We have not had a real night of sleep for some time and we know that they have it worse than we.

I have maintained excellent health all the time. Even with soaked clothes and irregular meals and sleep, this outdoor life has built up in all of us a tremendous resistance so except for the unpleasantness of it all, we suffer no real ill effects.

So far, I have managed to come through every engagement without a scratch. At least three times I have been so close that men about me have been instantly killed but for some reason God has seen fit to spare my life. Such experiences make a lasting impression upon one and you cannot but feel a deep responsibility to produce the results in life for which God saw fit to spare you. I do not expect to get another promotion in the army, as to do so, I would have to take some desk job and leave my men. I do not want that unless I am ordered to do it. Two weeks ago I was the first Chaplain in this Division to receive a Bronze [Star] Medal in recognition "of exceptional service while engaging the enemy." I'll be very proud to keep that.

Last Sunday most of my services were held under heavy artillery fire. Just as I was pronouncing the benediction at one of them, a shell landed just behind the house where we were gathered, killing a boy outside and showering all of us with broken glass. Fifteen minutes later as my driver was walking over to get my jeep, another shell landed fifteen feet behind him, picked him up in the air and threw him down on his stomach with such force that it knocked the wind out of him. Otherwise, his only injuries were a skinned knee and a scratch on the hand. Such experiences of close ones, are matters of regular occurrence and you live constantly on intimate terms with death. But knowing that your accounts are settled with God and man, it need cause no real concern. Whether He lives with us here or we live with Him there, need not worry us.

Now I must sign off for today. It is pouring again but I have found an abandoned chicken-coop which is serving today as my study. A ration box adjusted across the bars of the roost make a surprisingly fine typing table (if only the chicken lice do not carry the machine away before one gets through).

November 19, 1944 - Germany

Another Sunday. It has been a rugged weekend. I have been able to have only one service as all of my units have either been on the move or preparing to do so. The sun has been out today so the shooting has been terrific. The air corps too, has been on the job since early this morning.

We are now allowed to say we are in Germany although you have no doubt guessed it long ago. We have been meeting terrific resistance and there has been little progress in this sector. I've been under more artillery fire the last four days than at any time since reaching the continent. There is a tremendous roar on every side that seldom lets up. Most of it is our own guns, but the British are close by. As I am located in front of these big guns, we get the full benefit of the blast. The Germans have been sending plenty our way, too. I was ducking them for five solid hours yesterday.

Last night they plastered bombs all around us. I am sorry to say my assistant was hit. A piece of shrapnel the size of my little finger went through his thigh. It did not hit the bone and as it was a clean wound I hope it will soon heal. He was in good spirits as we loaded him into an ambulance to be taken to a hospital in the rear. Tomorrow I must write his mother and his wife. Two others of our men were injured by the same bomb and several of our vehicles wrecked.

So I think you can understand that I am very thankful to be hale and hearty tonight. God's protection of my life is a constant source of wonder to me. How well I know how undeserving I have been. I sincerely pray that my life in a fuller measure may show my thankfulness in the days to come. I know it was with a full heart that I read this evening Romans 8:31-39. It has become one of my favorites.

I was complaining to my boys here today that there just isn't an awful lot a Chaplain can do here these days as it is suicide to gather men in groups. So we can seldom have a service. But one of the fellows spoke up and said, "Chaplain, just seeing you around when the shells are flying, is a help."

Until now it has been practically forbidden for combat chaplains in this area to write letters of condolence to the families of boys who are killed in our outfit. However, folks at home have raised such a fuss at receiving only cold, official letters from the War Department that we are now instructed to write them. So now I have to go back through all the records since the day we landed, gather all the information I can, add such personal touches as I may know about each, and hope that this may serve to ease the pain a little.

November 24, 1944 - THANKSGIVING DAY, Germany

Another Thanksgiving is past. It really had some of the elements of a good U.S. celebration. We were all supplied with immense turkeys and we had all we could eat. Most units par-boiled them the day before so they were as tender as could be. The rest of the meal each unit had to rustle as best they could. Our cook wanted to make dressing so asked if I could find any onions. Well, I rummaged around in a few German cellars with a flashlight and soon returned with a bushel of them. But still no dressing - he had no sage and decided that gravy would be a good substitute. So we had turkey, gravy, mashed potatoes, green peas and hard candy for dessert. I found another unit which had cranberries but couldn't locate any with mince-meat pie-a-la-mode.

Of course, thousands of our men were sitting out in the rain and mud and had no facilities for cooking. But in most cases the turkeys were prepared in rear area kitchens and brought up to the men in great thermos containers. A few tried to prepare theirs over a fire of gasoline in a can.

I was unable to have a real service to commemorate the date, but I did go around from unit to unit, gun to gun, and gathered the men for a bit of God's Word and a Thanksgiving prayer. I waded in knee deep mud, soaked from head to foot, but the appreciation of the men as we bared our heads in the downpour to talk with God about our national blessings, His watch-care, and then in spirit joined the folks at home as they were gathered for their meal, was reward enough for even more misery than I suffered. I ministered to several hundred men and had twelve services.

I had planned much more, but I found so many of my units on the move that there was no opportunity. Besides, my day was cut short as the report came to me that in one of the areas where our men were to set up, there were several soldiers who had not been buried. I drove up there and found five of them. This is one service which I feel demands immediate attention. It is bad for the morale of the men to leave any unburied G.I.'s about. Besides, it runs contrary to my feelings of the respect to be shown those who have given their lives to leave them lie around until we have nothing else to do. By the time I had gotten a truck to haul them twenty miles to the rear, had gotten each wrapped in a blanket on a litter and had convoyed the truck to a grave collecting point where we checked each body for all necessary identification and had then driven back to my headquarters, it was still raining, pitch dark,

10:00 p.m. and I was dog tired. I hadn't even had a chance to eat supper. However, with the big dinner [lunch], I survived until breakfast without difficulty.

Today, our outfit is moving again. That will take about three hours and packing and unpacking the vehicle and getting a new bed set up will take the rest of the afternoon. So an awful lot of the week is wasted in this manner. No help for it.

Mail has been a sorry mess for a long time. Nothing coming through. But we read in our army papers that there is such a load of Christmas letters and packages that they can hardly handle it. That's good news and we'll wait for it.

November 27, 1944 - Germany

The eastern sky is streaked with gray as the sun is bravely trying to break through the overcast. If it succeeds, it will be the second day in a row that we have had no rain and a bit of sun. That would be a record. The temperature continues just about freezing. We're comfortable at night, though, as we have the remnants of a house for shelter and even a bit of a stove which we dug out of the debris.

We were up a good while before daylight today. We had scheduled a big attack and you never in your life heard such a commotion. I was out watching the cannons belching fire, listened to the angry whirr as they tore through the sky and then saw the impact in a great ball of fire. It would be really picturesque if it were not for the fact that you know that undying [immortal] souls are being hurled into eternity. I felt constrained, as I watched, to pray earnestly for the souls of both friend and foe who as the day dawned were being rushed into the presence of their Maker.

Yesterday was Sunday and I managed by rough driving and plenty of freezing to get in four services. Two of them were very well attended. One I held in a wrecked house and the other in the private chapel of a farm house. The other two services were held in a mine shaft, right up in the front lines. Only sixteen men were able to attend each of those services. It was miserably cold. Right by my ear on one side, one of our artillery guns pumped out fifteen shells right in the middle of the service. At my other ear, a big bull-dozer was snorting and grinding as it moved several tons of wreckage to clear a roadway. I finally ended up by getting my jeep stuck in mud up over the bumper. We had to leave it and walk the last mile to get a truck to pull us out. So ends the day.

December 6, 1944 - Germany [letter to daughter, age 11]

My dear Marilyn,

Today it is St. Nicholas Day in this part of Europe. In peace time they celebrate it just like we do on Christmas Eve at home. It is a problem for them in war time because they have had nothing to give the children. But I have had the great fun of helping about fifty families in Holland. I will tell you a little about it.

I heard about a week ago that they celebrated this day. So I went to my men and asked all who had any candy, gum or cookies that they would like to give to poor children, to bring it to a box for me.

The men have been getting Christmas boxes from home so they have more than they can eat. The army has been supplying us with a lot of candy also during Thanksgiving and afterward. In a few days I had gathered almost forty pounds of hard candy, sixty rolls of life-savers and about the same number of boxes of cookies and a hundred packages of gum.

All this I hauled to some Red Cross workers just over the border in Holland. They simply cried for joy. They had not had candy for four years and had been so troubled that they could not provide anything for the children this year.

So on Monday they divided it all up into parcels and went from house to house and handed it to the parents. The workers told me, "We cannot pay you for all you have done, and we have nothing to give you. But I will tell every family that they shall pray for the chaplain and the kind American soldiers every day."

So last night all the little children put their wooden shoes beside the chimney for St. Nicholas. Last evening they were busy scrubbing every speck of dirt from them and washing themselves until their faces shone. That is not the easiest thing either, as they have no soap. But after they get into bed the parents put the gifts in the shoes and you can be sure the children were there before it was light this morning. Besides the candy, they will probably find some doll clothes that mother has been able to make from some scraps of cloth and some wooden blocks and simple toys that father has made from scraps of wood.

So, Honey, if you feel a bit lonely on Christmas Day because your Daddy and brother are away, you just remember how much you have to enjoy that millions of children in Asia, Europe and Africa do not have.

I am well and happy and keep busy trying to cheer up the men who must live, eat and sleep in the mud and the cold. God bless and keep you.

December 23, 1944 - Christmas in the Ardennes, Forest of Belgium

If, when you receive this, you turn back to the events in Europe just before Christmas, I am sure you will realize our hands have been pretty full. We have been on the road again a great deal. These night marches without lights on slippery roads and in pouring rain are really something. For an entire day and night we did not even take time out to eat, much less sleep. But it is of greatest importance to be just where we are needed at the moment we are needed, so comforts and even necessities are not very important.

Against such a background, you can imagine what my feelings were last night when, instead of the frozen ground which I had expected, I found I was going to be able to sleep in the home of the town mayor. He guides the destiny of only a little village, so from the standpoint of influence, he would not be regarded as being very much. But the long line of blue blood which is attached to every public office, makes even small officials interesting characters.

How you would love to explore this massive house. It is a couple of hundred years old and the principle building on a large estate which has several tenant families taking care of the soil (and paying profits to the owner, of course). Well, the house has perhaps thirty rooms. The ceilings are fully 15 feet high. Drapes and tapestries from all over Europe and colonial possessions adorn arches and windows. The walls are literally hung like an art gallery.

The mayor having plenty of leisure, is able to indulge his hobby. This happens to be the preparation and mixing of oils for painters. He assures me that his oils are as fresh after 100 years as today. I'm inclined to believe him after seeing some of the art here for which his father supplied materials. So he spends most of his time in a factory which he has erected on the grounds, mixing oils. He has contact with famous painters from all over Europe. One enters a dream world as one comes through the door.

December 25, Christmas 1944 - German Breakthrough at Leige, Belgium

I should have an enthusiastic letter to write you about our Christmas activities. But I haven't. To be sure, we did make rather elaborate preparations. We had even cut down a tree, found some trimmings in wrecked homes, made lights out of flashlight bulbs, soldered to a wire and lighted by dry cells. I had even been authorized to spend 75¢ per man for a little gift. Then we had arranged for passes to take the men back to Holland (we were at that time in the Siegfried Line) as guests in about 200 homes. It was really planned to be quite a Christmas.

Instead, we spent the holidays in some of the bloodiest fighting we have seen on the continent. (Written from the Ardennes Forest, the so-called "Big Bulge.") It may well be that history will record that the action of our Division during this Christmas was one of the great crises of the war. As a result of this intense fighting, we did not even have a service. Our Christmas dinner was eaten out of tin cans on snow-covered hillsides.

Now the big push is over and we are permitted a breathing spell. We have fully two feet of snow here and the moving of our heavy equipment is a real problem. Having been engaged in combat so long, we will make good use of this time to repair vehicles, get ourselves rested and cleaned up. I also hope to be able to have a daily service in a saloon in the village here.

I am well and safe. My home at present is an immense factory. It is good protection as it is made of concrete and steel. We manage to keep dry as I even have a little stove. Really, I am doing very well but do not try to sell me a ticket to travel in Europe. When I have dug fox-holes in every cow pasture from the English Channel to Berlin, I not only want to "See America First," but last and always.

December 30, 1944

Today I write you from the office of a Catholic priest. What do you think of that? He has given my assistant and me a room here in his parish house and I have the use of his study for reading and writing. So, I shall have to be grateful to the Catholics for this much at least, that I have a roof over my head and congenial surroundings for a day or two.

I should add that we are not now pushing so hard on the line and I have hopes that I may be able to gather many of my men for church tomorrow.

The weather continues cold and we are glad of it. The ground is like rock and we are able to travel anywhere. We have nourishing food and good clothing so we will get along O.K. The Germans suffer worse. Yesterday I saw a number of prisoners. I was told that they were of crack German Panzer Divisions. They may have been well-trained and tricky, but they were certainly the sorriest specimens of men I have seen in a long time. Several were as hollow-cheeked as skeletons. None had shaved in days. Their uniforms were ill-fitting and several had on uniforms of our men. One had one overshoe of each kind. Their faces and hands (and I suppose the unexposed parts of their bodies as well) were broken out with sores and boils. I suppose this was largely due to exposure and malnutrition. They were pathetic. Supermen, bah. Why will a robust, healthy nation persist in years of warfare that sucks the life-blood out of its men?

Sunday P.M.

I'll have to give you some picture of the difficulties we have to put up with in arranging services for front line troops. I began yesterday investigating where I might find my troops for services today. As I told you, they are not so busy now so it is important to contact all I can.

So -- I inquire about A Battalion on Saturday at 4:00 p.m. No, they cannot be contacted because the telephone line has been pulled out and they are to move at 5:00 p.m. Well, how about B? They can be reached now but are to be on the road Sunday morning at 10:00 a.m. and do not know if they'll have any place to assemble. So I come to the end of the day with services arranged for C in the morning at 9:30 and for D at 1:00 p.m.

So this morning I start buzzing around again. There is still no line in to A. Because of icy roads, B is being delayed and will not reach their new area until late in the p.m. and it will take the rest of the day to get set up and find bedding for the men. No chance there. My 9:30 service gets started ten minutes late because I have to use the room where the officers eat and they were late. Some men cannot attend because they must haul gas, water, return pop bottles, get frozen vehicles started. So the attendance was nothing to brag about.

Then I had arranged for the men to take shower baths this p.m. and so before dinner drove several miles to make a last minute check to see that everything was O.K. It is well that I did. I found that the water pump had broken down and we could not take showers at all.

So right after dinner, I started off for my service at D. I was unable to reach their main building as all the trucks blocked the road. The first Sergeant tells me that they are ordered to pull out for 2:00 p.m. So that goes up in smoke.

However, I could perhaps arrange a service at this late hour in one of the other units by driving over there. But now my Adjutant reports that at 3:00 p.m. every officer must be present to be paid. When that is over, it's almost dark and it will be too late to go anywhere. So unless the Lord rewards His servants on the basis of honest effort and faithfulness instead of on the basis of success and accomplishment, here is one laborer in the vineyard who is definitely in the red for this Sunday.

Needless to say, it takes a good supply of optimism and good humor to meet with frustration of this kind. If one didn't care whether the men heard the gospel or not, it would not be a burden. As it is, the load gets a bit heavier at times than one can well carry.

Part III: 1945

January 3, 1945

I haven't written you anything in a long time about the country through which we travel. I think the one thing that has amazed me more than any other, are the many and large forests. I have always thought of Belgium and Holland as the "low countries" with marshlands and dikes. That is only true of the sectors near the ocean. In the interior, the country is really very much like Minnesota or upstate New York. There is a good system of improved roads, usually macadam, and we breeze along through towering forests which would be mighty picturesque were it not that too often there are Heinies lurking about. The trees include quite a number of familiar hardwoods but the biggest share are evergreen: spruce, pine, tamarack. These people are great on reforestation. Everywhere groups of young trees are growing. When they cut a tree, they do not saw it off and leave a stump of two to three feet. They use an axe and actually chop down below the surface of the ground by the time they get into the center of the tree.

The country has pretty good drainage for the most part and rushing brooks and small rivers criss-cross everywhere. Now that it has turned cold, the icicles hang from branches and the humps of rocks.

(This is as far as I managed to get last night. I was trying to write in a room with about ten other officers and GIs. They insisted that they were going to take a spiritual inventory of every man present on the basis of the Ten Commandments. Besides needing my help in an honest evaluation, they also had to have me quote the commandments. I'll admit it started out more as a game than any special heart-searching test, but it had possibilities. I let them give themselves a good score. They were quite honest and finally ended up with what they felt they had earned -- grades between 70 and 90. I then asked them what God's passing grade was. Well, they thought about 75 per cent so that should give almost all of them a pretty good chance. So I quoted from the Word that God says that "cursed is every man that continueth not in all the deeds of the law to do them." I said a Holy God demands nothing less than 100 per cent or you have flunked out. A Captain said he could not figure that out. Then they just didn't have a chance. I said that was just what God was trying to tell them: "As many as are of the deeds of the law are under the curse."

The air was pretty tense in the room by then and they were no longer playing a game. "But Chappie," said a Captain, "there must be something more that goes into the figuring." I answered, "There certainly is. Here is where the perfect life and the atoning death of Jesus Christ

133

come to our rescue." Then I had a chance to tell them as I've so often told them, but which never seems to become real until the Spirit under special circumstances gets a chance to drive it home, of Christ on the cross paying our penalty so that we no longer attempt by the hopeless medium of the law to be accepted by God, but by faith in Christ, "all who believe are justified from all things from which they could not be justified by the deeds of the law." It was a mighty interesting hour and I thanked God for it. But I did not get this letter finished as it was almost midnight when we had gotten to the end of our talk.)

This morning I look out upon a world with a fresh carpet of white. It has been snowing most of the night -- a wet heavy snow. The clouds now almost scrape the top of the buildings. It is beautiful but terribly wet for the infantry and the roads get packed and smooth as glass. In the murky overcast, the Germans counter-attacked twice early this morning, but we were there with more than enough to push them back.

Living Among Royalty

We are living for this day in another chateau. It is an immense affair. I understand the madam in charge is a countess. I haven't taken the trouble to find out. Purposely, she has filled several of the rooms with neighbors so we shall not use them. Another unit had been here before us and she was worrying herself into tears because they had left some dust and cigarette butts behind. No doubt combat troops ought to travel with O'Cedar mops and floor wax on their backs. We told her she had better be a bit more agreeable as we were no more anxious to be in this country than she is to have us here. Furthermore, it is entirely within our power to order her and the whole caboodle out of the place and take over every room in the place. I wouldn't be a bit surprised if she is a Nazi collaborationist. At least she has had the Germans here before and speaks very highly of them. Well, we'll be on our way presently. Maybe we should just have let the Jerries smash this thing to the ground. Then she'd have something more than dust to complain about.

But as to the house, it's quite an affair. There are perhaps twenty rooms in the house proper, and around it are the humbler houses of the tenants who work the place for her and the stables of fine cattle and Belgian horses. As in all of these chateaus over here, there are tons of massive antique furniture. Immense pictures (mostly landscape and hunting scenes) adorn all the rooms and staircases. There are also original paintings in oils, life-size, of all the heads of the family for generations.

The rooms are immense. We occupy the master bedroom. Some idea of its size can be gained from the fact that there are nine of us officers sleeping in there now. We still have room for an immense wardrobe closet in solid mahogany with three full-length mirrors, two tables, six chairs, bed tables, floor lamps and two dressers. Some shack. Her sewing room is as big as [sister-in-law] Hermina's parlor.

Now with this letter finished, I'm taking off in my jeep through the snow to find one of the units which has been doing the heaviest fighting in this position. I'll not be able to have services but a word here and there may come in the classification of Jesus' work when it is said of Him that He "went about everywhere doing good."

Most of all, I would love to have you to cherish and to hold. How much real understanding love would mean now.

January 12, 1945

It is bitterly cold here now. But for a native of the Northwest, it is invigorating and beautiful. If I had my way about it, I would be out tramping in the snowdrifts.

Needless to say, one must curb some natural tendencies and be constantly reminded that we are not on a hike but engaged in a death struggle. We are never allowed to forget that for long. Just yesterday one of our boys was blown to bits when he had taken off during his spare time to see if he could not find some rabbits. Instead, he stepped on a mine and that was that. I knew him very well. He was the first lad with whom I bowed my knees in this Division. I told you about him in Africa. How bitterly he wept for his sins and earnestly prayed that he might be forgiven and have strength to resist temptations. He gave his testimony on several occasions later and I talked with him on frequent occasions. Now he is beyond my power to help or Satan's power to hinder.

I had two services yesterday. In my present area there are the remains of a church. All the windows are gone and the furnishings are pretty much rubble. But in this sector, we are so crowded that one gladly settles for any kind of place that affords a roof and floor space enough to stand. I had 46 men at one service and 21 at the other. I served communion at the close of both services. It was so bitterly cold that I could hardly bend my fingers enough to administer the sacrament. If plans materialize, I may be able to have more frequent services under better circumstances now for a time.

My home for the present is not too bad. I occupy the second floor bedroom of a farmhouse, if you please. The bed has been reduced to kindling wood, but the mattress is still intact so it keeps me off the cold floor. I have no heat in the room but putting on twice as much clothes at night as I wear during the day, enables me to keep the blood stream in a liquid state. There is a hole six feet square in the one wall where an artillery shell came tearing through recently and where the snow now violates the privacy of our boudoir. My driver occupies the room with me and a good share of the time one must crawl over two or three more bundles of blankets containing weary hunks of humanity before one can get to one's own bed.

One of the hundreds of things that one really misses in the army is privacy. Men come and go constantly. It is an unwritten law that whether they have anything to say worth listening to or not, they can barge in and interrupt you at what you are doing. Very seldom do I even have a chance to pray in secret. Study and letter-writing are nightmares of interruptions. To be able to go to bed and sleep right through until morning will be paradise indeed. But here you have just dozed off and in comes someone flashing a light around the place and yelling that one of your room-mates is wanted on the phone, or is to go on guard, or must move his vehicle, or that they cannot find that document that the General wants right away. Or perhaps some guy has lost his way and is to stay until morning with us. So we are to shift our blankets around to make room for him. You know from bitter experience the mood that men are in when awakened all hours of the night and getting out onto an ice-cold floor and stumbling around in the dark certainly does not make for harmony in the family. But when morning comes you just forget it, as one of the many rotten things about this rotten war that is unavoidable or at least will never be remedied until we pull off this uniform for the last time.

January 19, 1945 - Belgium

Believe it or not, we're snowbound. For nearly 24 hours we've been having a typical North Dakota blizzard. Roads are blocked, vehicles are stalled, everything is frozen up. Yesterday at noon sleet started in, snapping off trees and branches as they became burdened with long icicles. Our phone lines were snapped one after the other and trucks going out to repair them were stuck in the drifts. The wind registered 60 miles per hour last night.

The double window in my room is out. There is no heat there but we did have quite a snowdrift there this morning. Today we're trying to keep from freezing to death by burning the green wood which is available. There is no draft in the chimneys, except in reverse, so our eyes burn with wood smoke and our feet have been freezing for days. But it's O.K. We are well, safe, eating hot food, enjoying the heart-warming assurance of dear ones who love us and that our God is our constant companion.

January 23, 1945

Each day I am caused to marvel at God's protecting care. I never understood why He chose to miraculously guard me as unworthy as I am. I must tell you of a recent experience even at the risk of making you even more keenly aware of the dangers faced daily in combat.

In an area we recently occupied, I told you in a letter that I had gone out and found the bodies of five G.I.'s. Now I must add that on the following day one of our motorcycle riders had to satisfy his curiosity by going out to see what I had found. Right in the area where I had been working, he stepped on a German shoe mine. His foot was mangled, his leg all the way up his thigh was chewed up with a dozen pieces of steel.

The next day, a major and four men who had been assigned the job of hauling the bodies out of there, were in the same area. One of the men stepped on another mine and his leg was brutally broken close to the knee. As he fell, one of the other lads rushed to his side to help him and he stepped on a third mine. His left foot was completely blown off.

Through this entire area, I had been working for more than an hour, digging bodies out of the snow and searching them for identification. Yet nothing happened. No wonder my men have been asking, Chaplain, do you have a charmed life?' "Do you call it luck or Providence when you escape without a scratch?"

You know of course what my answer is and I am given an excellent opportunity to witness to many who will never attend a church service. And yet, as I have told you before, I do not feel for a moment that the fact that I am a Christian entitles me to any immunity. Many better Christians than I have given their lives in this and other wars. So I can only marvel and praise God that He chooses in this way to magnify His Name through me.

January 30, 1945 - Enjoying a Rest Area, Belgium

Sunday was a good day. I had been having daily services last week. The attendance increased from 27 on Tuesday to 79 on Saturday. We met in a theater in the rear of a saloon. (It's the first time in my life that I have made posters to tack up outside a saloon to invite men to come in.) It's a good thing that the God who is no respecter of persons is likewise no respecter of places, but wherever men are come together in His Name, there He is in the midst of them to bless. And so we experienced it. Several men have indicated to me of late that they really know very little about the foundation of our Christian, evangelical faith. So I decided that now that I have a few days in which I can give a series of messages to approximately the same group, that I would begin a Bible study on what we believe and why. I used as a basis for our study, the three articles of faith contained in the Apostles Creed. There have been quite a number who have expressed their thanks for the help received. I remember especially one who came up to me after the service on Friday who said, "Chaplain, I surely do thank you for giving me for the first time a clear understanding of what the death of Christ means." I aimed at being both doctrinal and practical so the men would get food for thought as well as for the soul.

As we are having an intensive training schedule these days, a couple of movies daily, a dance and party at least once a week, shower trucks for men to go some distance to get cleaned up, it is no small task to find a time of day when a fair percentage of the men can come. As all of these activities (except the showers) are all held in the one heated building that is available in any area, the problem is complicated further. But I do have enough cooperation so I can get them, at least on Sunday, to juggle their schedule so as to make room for services. So on Sunday afternoon, I had arranged to have the 3:00 p.m. movie cancelled and I had the use of the theater for the service. I got word around to all of the units on Saturday and then went to the movie when it was almost over and while they were changing for the last reel, I asked for "quiet" and then announced that immediately following the show there would be a Protestant service. We had a very good turnout again. We had communion also after this service and I met a number of Christian lads I had not seen since England. By the time all this was over it was getting dark and I barely had time to get back to my own headquarters for supper.

At breakfast the next morning (yesterday) I accidentally heard that the office where Erling Tonnessen is working is just a few miles from here. It being "blue Monday" I found it easy to combine business with pleasure and drive down there for the afternoon and early evening. I found him in the very best spirits and enthused about my visit. He has a chance to follow our activities quite closely and he had been concerned about my safety, of course.

It happens that the place where he is staying is famous for mineral baths. Later I'll send you a picture of it. Of course, nothing would do but that we should try this out. It was an immense place. We paid 20 francs (about 45¢) and were given a private bathroom with a solid copper tub. This was almost filled with steaming, bubbling mineral water. It tastes and acts like carbonated water and is supposed to be very healthy. I soaked out about three weeks of dirt and then just lay there in indolent luxury until the clock on the wall said my time was up.

To wind the day up perfectly, Erling took my assistant and me to a restaurant where we had a delicious steak dinner with crisp, brown, fried potatoes and dark bread and butter. There were no salads, soup or beverage or pastry, but we had enough and I'm sure it cost Erling a week's pay. But he insisted we were his guests and it was his treat. It was certainly a perfect day and I hardly thought of the war from morning until night.

Boy, there's so much to write about today, I'll not get it all in this envelope I know. Last week I did get a landslide of mail. One day I had 25 letters. Most of them were Christmas cards of course, but just as welcome. I must have received at least ten from you. One evening I spent all the time from supper to bed-time reading mail. Besides your letters, I also received your 7-pound box of peanut squares. Are they habit-forming, like whiskey, do you think? I put them way up out of reach after I had consumed two rows of them and had decided to call a halt, but it does no good. I waste half of the time I'm sitting here by getting up and dragging them down. So I've just decided to let nature take its course and set the box right at my elbow and every time my mouth starts to water, I cast all rules of diet to the wind, and chew away as long as I'm in the room. The other box with my fish foods arrived, too. While we're in this rest area, we eat like kings, really, so it is only common sense to save some of these luxuries until we're in the field again. I have only fallen once, to the extent of consuming (with very little help from others) one of the big boxes of sardines. The rest of the treasure is intact.

I believe I told you that I was to get my other assistant (who had been wounded) to work with me again. I must tell you that he has returned a changed man. I am thrilled to the depths of my soul. He had been a Christian when first he entered the army and had taken an active part with Christian soldiers. But had drifted and had become very worldly. He continued in the Chaplain's section but his heart was in the Special Services where they worked for dances and parties and movies. The very first night he was with me last week, I noticed that he had laid his Bible out on the window sill. I worked rather late and he went to bed but I noticed that he did not sleep. So I finally said, "Russell, you haven't told me anything about your trip to the hospital. How did you make out?" So he began to tell me of how it had made a complete change in him. That you see things differently when you honestly face the issues of life and death. He said he had never completely turned away from God, but the thing that made it real to him of how far he had drifted was the fact that a soldier who lay next to him in the hospital had actually asked him if he could show him how to be saved and he could not. He said he was so convicted that he turned to God for mercy and pleaded to be restored. He was. He said he had not in two years known the inner peace and freedom from strain and tenseness which had been his for two years. Now he wants to study for the ministry and I think he would do well. He has a good mind and the most winsome personality. I'm going to help him get lined up with a Bible School.

We had just gotten nicely started when his name came up for a few days pass in Paris. So now he is gone again. I'm glad he had a chance to go. I may never get a chance to go there myself. It's not a matter of life and death, but I certainly would like to see the place, particularly the cathedrals and art museums before I leave Europe. Now in my assistant's place I have gotten a lad from one of the firing batteries who is a real Christian. He has welcomed the chance to be where he has leisure to study God's Word (he has attended Moody [Bible Institute] one year) and to attend services daily. He plays the organ a bit and does my driving as well as run errands for me.

So, my honey has blossomed out in a fur coat this winter. Good for you. I am not sure that it was an accident or on purpose that you made a typographical error in writing the price. But anyway, you had typed the figure over twice so I couldn't read what it was. Now I do not know what you paid. But I'm not worried. You've never squandered money on clothes and when we can afford it I want you to look attractive as well as to be warm. All I ask now is that you send me a good picture of yourself in it.

Since most letterwriters begin with a discourse on the weather, I will close this with a weather report. We are having snow practically every day. The snowplows are kept busy keeping the roads open. It is the most beautiful crystal white and I enjoy it. I go stomping through the white blanket up to my knees during the day and then at night return to my warm bed. The bracing air and biting wind have no terrors when one is well clothed and healthy. And I'm both. To God be the praise for all His temporal and spiritual gifts.

February 3, 1945 - Belgium

I was thinking as I awoke this morning, how our life in the army is like that of Abraham of whom it is said that he "obeyed, and he went out, not knowing whither he went." But just as his uncertainty is like ours, so is also the assurance that God was with him to lead, protect and bring him to his destination. Sometimes for a day or two life becomes so routine that one could almost think there was no war. But then, without advance notice, often with the greatest secrecy, comes "March Order!" and off we go again.

I've been making good use of our stay here. Yesterday I left our headquarters at 9:30 and did not get back until 8:00 p.m. I visited six units, gave out about 800 tracts, conducted a service and talked to any number of lads. It was a blessed day.

After almost a month, or perhaps more, of real winter, we have the last two days been having a genuine spring thaw. Practically all the snow is gone. Our friend, mud, is with us again and every ditch and valley is a gurgling torrent of water. I'm sure it's too early for it to warm up for good, but even the air feels like real spring.

Once again the clouds are lifting for the Allied cause. Just think that this Russian advance has been pounding on for 300 miles without a stop. That is uncanny. Today you could drive a jeep from the Russian lines to Berlin in 45 minutes. The starving and frantic millions of civilians within the city can hear the guns of the Russian advance. After what was done to their own civilians, Germany can expect nothing else from these godless Russians than the worst barbarism and atrocities in the annals of history. This the Germans surely know. How they then can keep on fighting without sueing for peace is a mystery. Is not defeat better than annihilation?

March 3, 1945 - German Civilians

We are now in an area of Germany where many civilians have been left as their armies have retreated toward Berlin. In the larger places they are without food and come begging to our mess lines for scraps. The old people and children are especially tragic. We are not allowed to even speak to them, of course. Many of them are of the families of German soldiers and it is quite a sight to see them gather around the cages where we keep the prisoners whom we have been herding in by the hundreds all this week. The folks want a last word with their men before they are sent away but that is out of the question. One is constantly in danger of letting one's Christian sympathy get the better of one's judgment. But if you do, our lads are going to pay for your indiscretion. I have seen these same contrite and weeping women gnashing at us with their teeth. They would put a knife into our backs just as quickly as a soldier would. The only solution is strict discipline.

You were inquiring about our taking over civilian homes to live in and stating that you understood that was the German and Russian way of doing things. Well, I do remember the many months when these people lived in their fine homes with heat and light while we who had given up every joy in life to travel 3000 miles to set their country free, had to eat, work and sleep in the mud, soaked to the skin day and night. They had immense air-raid shelters while we had to dig out slit trenches in the rock and tree roots while enemy planes overhead were strafing away.

Well, we kept this up until men's lives were lost, others developed pneumonia and other respiratory diseases that curtailed our effectiveness. Still we stayed out in our pup tents during the winter until we froze so at night that we had to get up every hour to run around to stimulate circulation. And all the while these people were living in their comfortable homes.

Our leaders finally put some sense into this nonsense and had the people move into a few rooms of their houses while we occupied the rest.

The Germans and Russians in their offensive had required all of the civilians to retreat with their own armies or be interned in camps. That is cruel and we'll never resort to it. But it accomplishes two things. With all the civilians on the roads behind the lines it makes it all the more difficult for the retreating army to get away. Besides, these millions of aged, women and children constitute a tremendous burden in feeding, clothing, sheltering and medical aid. It should be the Germans' job to take care of their own population. But as it is, the army retreats and the civilians are left behind. After the tide of battle has passed them, they come out from hiding. Their rickety carts clutter up the highways which are the life-lines of supply to our troops. Many of them are spies in civilian clothes. Their presence requires us to investigate each and every one of them. This consumes thousands of hours of precious time and hundreds of essential military men. Then their homes are ruined, they have no food, their machinery is destroyed so they cannot work their farms. Malnutrition takes its fearful toll in disease that taxes the time and facilities of our hospitals and aid stations which are essential to care for our own wounded and dying.

This will give you some idea of the realistic problems that must face any army which tries to be human and humane in its relations. It takes a keen sense of the sacred rights of human life to even tackle the problem. But even then, working it out is almost an insurmountable obstacle.

I have spent half of my forenoon dealing with civilians. I have actually learned a few words of German and when they speak slowly I can catch the drift of most of what they are after. So the Colonel said this morning, "You are hereby appointed mayor of this town. All these civilians are your problem." No one wants the job. I certainly do not. The mayor part was only a joke but the work is not. All morning they've been coming to our door. One wants permission to go to the neighboring town to get a cow that has run away. Another has a sick baby; will I get a doctor. Another has given their blankets to a wounded civilian that was sent to the hospital yesterday when some artillery shells landed in our area, so will I give them some bedding as they have nothing for their bed. An aristocratic family shows me a letter from the Swedish Counsel stating that they are good people and have a home in a city we have captured some forty miles from here. They fled to this village during the fight but now want a truck to haul all their belongings and themselves to their own home. They are unhappy and crowded in their present quarters, they say. (Do you think we are happy in ours?) Well, that's war. There's a lot more to it than pulling a trigger, you see.

March 7, 1945 - The Watch on the Rhine

I think the war front could well compete with the home front in optimistic predictions about the end of the war these days. I heard a report today that the War Department had announced that it would be all over in Europe in two weeks. Well, fine. Who am I to disagree. Nothing would make me happier. But I'm not packing my bag. I've heard these rumors come and go for a year now. I refuse to get my blood pressure up about it.

But there is certainly no denying that the tempo of our advances has increased these last weeks. With continued good weather the air force will be kept pounding day and night and our tanks are free to maneuver according to preconceived plan.

Meantime men continue to return to the States on rotation. One of our captains who was the first to land in Africa left for home and his wife this morning. One of my favorite 1st Sergeants also left. Before he took off, his commanding officer called the company together and made a little good-bye speech. He started off well enough to thank them for all their cooperation, to express his joy in leaving for home. But that's as far as he got. He broke down completely and wept unashamed. God bless him. Those were manly tears and I'm proud of him for it.

The outstanding event in my life this past week was unquestionably the opportunity to hear Lily Pons and her husband Andre Kostalonis. He directed an orchestra of fifty of the best musicians in two armies in this area. The former accompanist of Nelson Eddy, a Mr. Paxton, was the concert pianist. His performance of the Warsaw Concerto and the Blue Danube were superb. Lily Pons sang six numbers. She's certainly not much to look at, is she. Her wardrobe on the tour must be very limited, too, because though she appeared three times, she wore the same costume at all of them. Of the orchestra numbers, I personally enjoyed a group of Victor Herbert's numbers the most. You know my musical education leaves a good deal to be desired in the way of interpretation and appreciation of classical music. Herbert's is just about my speed. I should have mentioned in connection with Lily Pons' singing, that she is still mighty fine as a coloratura soprano. She sang all opera (light) numbers. She sang one "Ave Maria" but it was not the one I like best. Her rendition of "Hark, Hark, the Lark" gave her full opportunity to demonstrate both range and versatility. All in all, it was the most culturally uplifting two hours I have spent since I left the States. The German theatre which seated perhaps 10,000 was jam-packed to the doors. Even in the army there is an element that is interested in something besides shows.

March 15, 1945

Would you believe it -- here along the Rhine we actually had a game of volleyball this evening. It has been a beautiful day with sunshine and spring in the air. The farmers have been out in their fields turning the wet soil. Housewives have been hanging out their wash and bedding. Overhead, the bombers have been keeping up a steady drone for hours. Our artillery is lobbing shells across the river at targets of the enemy. With our troops making one bridgehead after the other across the Rhine, their artillery has been kept so busy working on them that they have had little left over to shell us here. Accordingly, we've been enjoying ourselves a bit.

I have taken quite a few feet of film today. Mostly farm scenes. They are really primitive. I've taken some fine scenes of oxen plowing and refugees returning to their homes, with vehicles of every description tottering under the immense loads. I even saw some little girls sitting on the sunny side of the house with their dolls and having tea. Why, you'd think we were miles from the war. But just now I hear the thud of incoming shells not very far away, so I know.

The mail today was funny. You no doubt have read of a shipload of Christmas mail that had been stopped four times and just now has reached the continent. Well, we got it today. My share was four Christmas cards -- arriving just about in time for Easter. Two letters from you dated December 5 and 7. One from [son] Bob about the same date. Naturally, it was all very old except the assurances of your love which are always as fresh as a blooming garden.

Your Valentine box came yesterday in the very best shape. I've been eating candy and cookies now until I'm ashamed of myself.

It is positively forbidden even to speak to a native here except in the execution of your military duties. That's a real hardship on the gay blades who feel called upon to make passes at every woman they see. It's even inconvenient for the many others who are interested in knowing how people think and feel. Even as Chaplains, we are not allowed to speak to the local clergy except for the purpose of arranging for the use of their churches. If we do this, the German people are not allowed to attend the same service with the soldiers. We are not even permitted to greet little children or give them things. It sounds pretty silly, no doubt, and many soldiers are mad as hornets about it. But they are usually the ones who are in need of just such restrictions to keep them out of trouble.

March 21, 1945

"Count your many blessings -- and it will surprise you what the Lord has done." Now ain't that the truth! I feel tonight that I have so much to be thankful for that my soul is bubbling over.

It's the first day of spring. Oh, it's been a glorious day. The buds have begun to burst. Farmers everywhere are digging in fields and gardens. Mothers and older sisters are out with the baby in the carriage. The farmyard poultry are cackling away contentedly. Bedding and winter clothing are hanging out the windows and from every clothes-line.

I've today made real progress on the job of supplying ice cream for 5000 men. I've had to make a round trip of 140 miles over lousy roads but seeing them in the mess line tonight going after it like ten year old kids, was worth all the trouble. I believe I told you that this sort of thing does not officially come within the category of a Chaplain's required duties. It rather belongs under the heading of going "the second mile" of which Jesus spoke.

Then this evening I had a service for my most unresponsive outfit. To my pleasant surprise, 32 men turned out for a mid-week service. We sang songs about the cross and I spoke on "Not my will but thine be done" from Jesus' prayer in the Garden. One of my Lieutenants sang a solo.

March 31, 1945

> "We don't have bacon
> We don't have bacon
> But we do have a piece of the Rhine."

And a mighty big piece it is, too. For days we have been thundering ahead without taking time to eat or sleep. And everybody is happy to endure these privations as long as we can keep on rolling.

Two weeks ago it would have seemed a fairy tale that we would be in this spot by Easter Sunday. Also that so many of our men would be spared to see another Easter. Now there appears to be no way of gathering to publicly thank God for the victories won but I do believe not a one of us fails to acknowledge to Him our gratitude.

I cannot tell you just when or where we crossed the Rhine, but after the days of softening up by the air corps and artillery, we all began, all along the line, to get units over. Some resistance was encountered, of course, but nothing like I had expected. We even found entire cities of several hundred thousands, completely evacuated of troops before we got there.

I have now seen what I had hoped these people would have sense enough to do months ago. They have let us enter and pass through towns without even a window pane being broken. Truckloads of prisoners are always passing down the highways. Everyone is a soldier of French, Polish, and Russian allegiance who has been driven into German slave camps, now trudging wearily down the roadsides, clothed in rags, and God only knows what they find to eat. They are all trying to make their way to the rear and ultimately home. The accumulation of miles we have travelled since crossing the Rhine is a figure almost unbelievable. But with hundreds of thousands of troops using only a few roads, we do not travel very fast and stops are frequent. So to make up the mileage, we must be driving day and night. We catch a half-hour of sleep occasionally and manage to get along. Enthusiasm makes up for loss of almost everything else -- temporarily, of course. The reaction will come, but we'll concern ourselves about that then. In the meantime we'll have to excuse infrequent letters, and those will be disjointed. But you will be praising God with us for the increased hope of a speedy end of this struggle and of blessed reunion.

April 11, 1945 - Germany

After eating little else than dust all day, I'm going to write a few lines. (Only this is as far as I got one-half hour ago, as a whole drove of Jerry planes came over and we've been blasting away at them like madmen. As far as I could see they only had a chance to drop one rack full of small bombs.)

I started out to say that having washed up and having eaten the first food since 5:00 a.m. (it is now 7:30 p.m.) I feel pretty good. The sun is just setting in a haze of smoke and dust. The artillery fire today has been terrific and we'll no doubt have a busy night. We have moved three times today and have advanced quite a few miles. About noon we approached a good-sized city where the enemy evidently have quite a few guns. So we follow our usual tactics of pulling off the roads into the fields, set up our guns and proceed to pulverize the town. Great fires will be burning all night. By morning, no doubt, scores of Jerries will have been killed, their guns blasted, the civilian homes smoking ruins, and we roll on our way to the next place they put up a resistance.

Not all towns are destroyed. Where they decide to surrender, we leave them unmolested and push on through. In the village where we have set up for this night, there is not even a window pane broken.

Did I tell you about the place we stayed over Sunday? One wealthy farmer seemed to own half the village and had the families there tilling his land which lay on all sides of the town. He had ninety pedigreed Holstein cows, two beautiful bulls, twenty-six immense oxen, eighteen work horses and three tractors.

They were Lutherans. They have had three sons, one of whom was killed in Russia and another in France. The third had come back from the fighting in Belgium with his right arm shattered by machine gun fire.

Slave Laborers

Besides their regular tenants and hired help, they must have had at least forty Poles and Russians working there. Some had been there as long as four years. Now they were free but because of the women and children, they could hardly leave in the cold, the congested roads, without food or money, and hardly knowing in what direction to turn for the road home.

They were always anxious to tell us their story. It was usually one of hardship and misery. The highest wage paid any of them was $6.00 per month. But even this was worthless as they were issued no ration coupons so could purchase nothing. They were given moldy black bread, half-rotten potatoes and a little milk for the small children.

Needless to say, the Germans are now worried sick about what these foreigners will do to them by way of revenge. Just this morning one who could speak some English came to say that we ought to leave some soldiers to defend the property owners from thievery and violence. I told them we did not bring these people here and it might have been well for them to think of the consequences in the days when they were arrogantly swinging the whip.

April 13, 1945 - Germany

A few lines again today will let you know that I am well and still pushing on toward our goal. We have during the past days cut, by more than half, the remaining distance to Berlin. We have done little more (as far as the artillery is concerned) than drive during the day, adjust our guns in the evening, spend the night shooting and sleeping, and then hitting the road again by dawn. Yesterday we advanced 28 miles before 9:00 a.m. The day before, we travelled about 30 miles in blinding dust all day. Generally, we get a chance to thoroughly clean up once a day and we are now getting at least one hot meal.

The casualties continue light, for which we praise God. However, each day brings some tragedy. Yesterday one of our cycle riders whom I've known so long, was killed. The day before, one of our half-tracks got a direct hit and burned like a firecracker. All six men in it were injured. One may not live, as he lost both legs. Another lost a foot. A third, the son of a pastor (it was his mother who sent us so many fine books in England) was badly burned. A Major got a bad cut over his eye. Etc.

Some interesting incidents transpire each day. I slept little last night, as the window to my room opened on the highway. In almost a steady stream, French P[O]W's whom we freed yesterday were marching back to join their own troops. It was a motley crew, but there was hope in their faces.

I have just finished finding a house to shelter some twenty Poles (most of them women) who have been working on this farm as slave laborers for four years. We sent the German out of his house. We cannot have them around or he will blow us all up even if he kills himself doing it. He is permitted to return twice a day with a hired man to care for the stock. The Poles were hungry and very poorly clothed. I found a house nearby occupied by only one German. I let him stay in the basement and installed them in the rest of the house. It will do no harm to turn the tables for the few days our troops are here. They wanted to stay at this place and wash and help feed us. But we have no room and besides, it is a serious problem to have these women around a group of men.

I wish you might have seen those women when I brought them into a house. For four years they've been sleeping on straw in stables and miserable barracks. They first stood in speechless wonder, then stroked the furniture with affection. One woman (I suppose she is hardly 40 years but with four teeth missing she looked 60) began to cry and stroked my face saying over and over, "Americans good."

You'd laugh until you were in stitches to hear me talk to these natives. Using my hands, facial expressions, pidgin English, a good percentage of imagination, and about twenty words of German, I understand and make myself understood. I've come to be regarded as the official interpreter and the solver of problems with the civilians. Most problems relate to property, separated families, requests for permission to travel and the fear of the plunder and violence of the slave Russians and Poles. To this last I give them little comfort. Aside from letting them take the food they need for their undernourished bodies, we keep looting down to a minimum while we are in the area. As to guarantees of what will happen as we leave and move forward, I tell the Germans that is their problem. We did not bring these foreigners here. They have worked them and abused them for four and five years. Now they may have to take the consequences.

Yesterday we captured a prison camp of 340 British soldiers. Many of them had been in prison as much as five years. The Germans had been working them in Poland until last January digging tank traps and building roads. Then as the west front took on importance, they marched them on foot, in the winter cold, for 19 days to Hildesheim. For food they were allotted one small loaf of black bread each day per three men and three potatoes each. Twenty-eight men died of exhaustion and exposure on the way. Then as we crossed the Rhine, they were pushed east again but finally their guards decided we were getting too close so they fled at night. The prisoners then simply waited until we reached them. We contacted the British forces and trucks arrived to bring them to their own troops.

This morning at 1:30 the electrifying news of the President's death reached us by radio. It was a terrific shock. It is a tremendous loss to our peacetime post-war cause. As the Vice President steps in, he lacks all the confidence, experience and prestige which F.D.R. has earned among our allies.

May 7, 1945 - GERMANY SURRENDERS!

I'm sure I must be running a fever these days. Events are transpiring with such speed as to make your head swim. Tonight's radio assures us that the Germans surrendered unconditionally to Eisenhower today and that official announcement will be made of this world-shaking event at 3:00 p.m. tomorrow. So it is over at last. The guns on the western front are to be silent at last.

Just what are my emotions at an hour like this? Frankly, I'm surprised at myself and I think a bit ashamed, too. Should I not be at my wits end with excitement? Should I not be walking on air? And I'm not. In one word, I believe I can best describe my feelings by saying I feel a great sense of relief. Perhaps it's because I'm tired. Maybe it's because we yet have no assurance as to when we will get home and that is the event we long for with such a passionate longing. Surely it is wonderful that lives shall not be sacrificed further even if we must still stay for some time. We cannot praise God enough for that. But somehow I do not get the emotional lift that will be mine when we walk up that old gang-plank and our ship heads for New York.

I haven't felt much like working today. I simply put in too hard a day yesterday. I started at 7:00 a.m. and finished at 9:30 p.m., having driven some over 100 miles (most of it in pouring rain), held five services, sang in five duets, led 15 congregational hymns, and preached five sermons. My voice was all in and my body really ached with weariness. I didn't sleep well, either. So all in all, I felt like loafing today and it was a perfect day for just that.

But I must add that I had a wonderful time. Two services were held in picturesque Lutheran churches, two in theatres and one in a saloon. The men really turned out so I had good attendance.

My favorite text was based on the good news which this past week had occasioned so much joy and cheering. "Three Good Cheers" which you will find in: 1) Matthew 9:2 - The Good Cheer of Forgiveness. 2) John 16:33 - The Good Cheer of Ultimate Triumph. 3) Mark 6:50 - The Good Cheer of Christ's Assured Fellowship. I think the outline scarcely indicates the line of thought which proved to be both heart-searching and interesting.

They have really been sprucing us up here these last days. I've had my jeep all painted today. We've had our helmets painted with our insignia which appears on this stationery and all men who were short items of uniform have been supplied. Now we are ready for almost anything. Let's hope it means a triumphant march to the sea to get on a boat for home.

I've just had a carpenter making a new case for my harp. I had wanted to keep the old battle-scarred case, but it is completely falling apart so the harp would be ruined.

Now I must see the Colonel to see what we can arrange by way of observance of V-E Day. I suppose they have in mind only to get in a shipment of liquor to celebrate the occasion but we'll have to remind them that God should get in for a bit of recognition.

June 6, 1945 - D-Day

A year ago today our forces stormed the beach at Normandy. The long-awaited hour for the opening of the Second Front had struck. It was by all odds the most difficult military maneuver ever attempted in the history of modern warfare. Landing through mine-filled sea lanes, 4000 warships and merchant ships disgorged thousands of tons of material and hundreds of thousands of men. 7,000 of those men died there on the sand and their bodies rest today beneath straight rows of white crosses on a hill overlooking that same beach. On the third day, I landed on that same beach. We lay in the shallows overnight while flak from Jerry planes and our own ack-ack [sic] rained like hail on the steel plates over our heads.

We've come a long way since then. We've "sweat out" many a sleepless night, many more nights and days we've plodded through rain and mud, dust and snow, constantly pushing until today sees the war in Europe ended and all its peoples set free. Looking at our day by day progress, I cannot say that I dared hope it would all be over within a year. When I thought about the end of the war, I cannot other than say I never doubted that I would still be hale and hearty to the very end. In fact, there were mighty few who faced each new day with any foreboding. Men were being killed, many of them. You might be next. But somehow it did not seem real even when you were hit. A healthy human mind is a remarkable mechanism when faced with a real crisis. You surprise yourself.

July 3, 1945

Once again the rainy season has set in here and they tell us it will continue for two months. I really wonder if they have any summer in Europe. We've never had more than two or three days at a time. Most of the time it is cold enough to wear a wool jacket even though we wear wool shirts and trousers. Take me back to the good old USA.

But I hardly dare mention coming home. I got a letter from you this morning and you seem to think that I'll be coming in by the next subway. I should never have built up such hopes. But the fellows all tell me that their families are the same way so I guess it's not entirely what I've written but largely what you hope for that has painted such a hopeful picture. Well, I'm coming just as fast as I can. If that's not fast enough to suit you, I can only comfort you by saying it doesn't suit me any better.

Through much of this country where we have passed, the Russians are to occupy. The Germans make no secret of the fact that they are frightened to death. Many have said they will commit suicide when the Reds come. No doubt their conscience reminds them that they have no right to expect any consideration. Just what the situation will be, it is too early to say. I am told that where they have good leadership, the discipline is pretty good. Otherwise, they are like wild barbarians with only one fixed idea: These are the people who plundered our land and slaughtered our defenseless people. When you remember that they have the morals of animals and most of them have been reared in an atmosphere of total atheism, it will not be surprising if there will be in some sectors a reign of terror.

We were still in some of the areas when the advance parties of the Russians arrived. They pasted stickers in shop windows notifying the people that they were not to leave their homes. This was necessary, as many would load up what they had and flee to a British or American sector if they could, and the highways would become impassable and the food and lodging problem impossible. Then they would put up large red banners across streets with the words: "The German people welcome the victorious Red army and their glorious leader, Joseph Stalin." The only hitch is that the Russians put them up, not the Germans. Many people got out bits of red cloth which they hung out their windows. Poor people. One day they are cheering Hitler, the next it is the Americans, and now it is the Reds. They are largely victims of circumstances which it is difficult to say to what extent they are responsible for.

Men Leave for Home

Well, we've had two busy days this week. First of all we awoke Monday morning to be informed that a whole batch of men were being sent home. We knew nothing of it in advance, but it spread like wildfire and in no time at all, every man-jack was figuring out his chances and griping about not being included. It is the first big bunch we have sent, so it has been a wonderful thrill. I get such a bang out of seeing them take off that I'm like a kid. I make it a point to contact each of them, get the name of their pastor and address of their church, and write him a letter. I have really had some touching experiences with these fellows as they take off. They will never return to the outfit and most likely we will never meet them again. We have passed through so much together that the bonds are ever so much closer than one would ever hope to establish normally in such a short time. As busy as they are, getting ready, some have taken time to call me and even to come to see me. In this batch almost two hundred men left from the Artillery.

Then are you ready for a real good rumor? Well, here it is -- and you know as well as I that army rumors can go up in smoke overnight. But today the Division Chaplain told me, "Well, Walstad, within 60 days you'll be on your way home, too."

July 4, 1945 - Arrival in Berlin, Germany

We've really had a day of it as we have just gotten settled in the quarters which are to be our home while in Berlin. I hardly dare describe our place to you or you will think I have gone so highbrow I'll not be fit to live with. It is certainly some contrast to the miserable nights we spent in foxholes and pup-tents. So perhaps this present luxury is our compensation for that misery. Well, now with that as a preamble, I can tell you that they assigned me a suite of rooms on the second floor of a large house. It has running water and lights. I have six (yes, I mean six) rooms -- a kitchen, two bedrooms, a study, a parlor and a private bath. It is all furnished so I have a good bed, comfortable chairs, desk and parlor lamps. Added to all this I have a sun porch, too. I can hardly believe it is real. They say we are to be here two weeks, so I will have a while to enjoy it, too. Last night I got only two hours sleep so tonight I'm prepared to just pass out.

I must tell you a little about our trip to Berlin. As usual, we were given an hour to start so we had everything packed. Then the hour was postponed for three hours so we were to start at midnight. Then about 11:00 p.m. we were told we might as well go to bed as they did not know what hour we'd be getting marching orders. Well, they finally got us out at 5:00 a.m. It was overcast and cold with occasional squalls of rain. We started on the super highway and followed that for about ten miles. Then a number of bridges were out so we had to start detouring all over the country -- an 80 mile trip got to be about 150. Our whole Division was on the road and it stretches out for 25 miles so you can understand the many halts and delays. But we did make the entire trip by daylight.

Meeting with the Russians

By far the most interesting part of the whole trip was the Russians we saw along the way. My description will not do them justice by any means. I can think of nothing that could possibly humiliate and bring the shame of defeat home to these arrogant, uniform-proud Germans as to see these columns of rag-tag Russians who whipped them. I've never seen a band of gypsies look worse. They have only one uniform in which they work, sleep, march and fight. It is a light color and so soiled you cannot even guess what the material is like. Like the German army in the last stages of the war, the men represent great extremes in age. I saw many marching men with white hair and beard and boys who had not even begun to shave.

Another thing -- their vehicles. Their trucks are the most decrepit looking things you've seen. Almost every one that is running is pulling one that won't run. They are loaded with all kinds of junk that hangs out over the sides. But most of their equipment is pulled by horses. We passed one convoy of horse-drawn material that was fully two miles in length. Most of the horses are skinny and look completely used up. The men are mostly quite cheerful though a number have, through all this bloodshed, developed an expression of sullen bitterness. Some units are of rather fine build and look intelligent. But many are from the mountains of Siberia, look like Mongols and Asiatics. Many of their faces hardly register intelligence.

The biggest surprise of all was to see all the women with them. They are piled into wagons and trucks with the men. Many were laying in heaps sound asleep with their clothes all crumpled and their hair a tangled mat. They used them not only as companions, but they fight with the men. I saw a number of them doing guard duty with a rifle across their shoulder. I have seen several of the women officers. They looked neat and capable. Their complexion was good and they had even added the feminine touch of rouging their lips. Needless to say, the comments by our men on seeing this version of modern war, have been varied and rather shocking.

Into the part of the city which we have come to occupy, the Germans are tickled that we have replaced the Russians. We are not allowed to associate much with them but they find ways of letting us know how delighted they are at the change. No doubt, there will be some disillusionment on the part of a number of them before we have been here very long, as our lads are far from angels. But I certainly can understand the relief which the rank and file of them feel. Not only are our morals better, but the Reds naturally have some very expeditious means of disposing of any who prove to have any Nazi leanings and who fail to cooperate with the Stalin brand of freedom.

July 5, 1945 - The Ruin that Once was Berlin, Germany

Since I wrote you this morning, I have had a chance to visit a good deal of Berlin. We only drove the streets without stopping so took in quite an area. It is a wreck. I could not help but think: "What would Times Square look like in this shape?" Really, our bombers have left such a mass of rubble that it is as though you are viewing the ruins of some ancient civilization rather than a scene of desolation where the bodies of the dead are hardly cold. Almost by any road you enter the heart of the city, it seems they have been fighting desperately. Wrecked tanks and ack-ack guns litter boulevard and streets. A large share of the buildings have been burned out so only four walls remain. But for the most part even the walls have crumbled under the weight. There is a river and several canals running through the city. Most of the bridges over these have been knocked out and only a few essential ones have been replaced by temporary ones. As a result, you frequently have to drive several miles to get to a place which is only a few yards away. Buses are running on several of the streets which have been cleared. I understand they have had a good subway system, but I could not find out if any part of it was still in working order. The amazing thing is that they have electricity. That seems to indicate that all their power plants were located far from the city and all power cables must have been buried far underground to withstand the raids.

All of the downtown sector is controlled by the Russians. There are quite a number of officers about and they greet us cordially. Their language is impossible, however, and I'm not even going to try to learn it. Not a single syllable makes sense. A unique part of their system is their use of girls as traffic cops in all the busy downtown intersections. Their uniforms are not much, but they are certainly efficient. They use a red flag in one hand and a white in the other. These they wave as a Boy Scout does semaphore, and then, seeing you are an officer, they dexterously shift both flags to the left hand and manage to salute you with the right before you have crossed the intersection.

All the people here complain about hunger. Farms about are hauling vegetables, especially carrots and cabbage. At the markets, long lines of people stand waiting in sun or rain. Quite a number of people appear quite well clothed as I understand there was a terrific amount of looting of stores after every raid. But you can't eat cloth. Each little sector of the city has its mayor who is hounded day and night by the problems of his people. It is certainly pretty rugged. It would be a real temptation for our soldiers to steal food from our kitchens to feed some of these folks but they have limited us to where we have barely enough ourselves. We have not eaten so poorly in a long time. I'm sure we have enough to give energy for the amount of work that has to be done, but when you have developed the kind of appetite that our outdoor life creates, it takes a while to adjust yourself to an office chair appetite again.

July 9, 1945 - Berlin, Germany

I have now gotten another assistant so we are three of us here. The army has authorized us to take in any young man who plans to go into the ministry and give him such practical training and study as is practical. I have asked for a lad from the South, Fred Latch. He is a sterling Christian lad, has only [a] high school education and is married. He is a Baptist and has some real ability as a speaker as well as a very likable personality. I enjoy having him live with me and he and Hartfield have been pals all through the war, so you can imagine what it means to them.

The mail is still hopeless. I'm even wondering if you get my mail. I understand that all plane transportation is already being tied up for this Big Three Conference to be held here soon.

I was able to get a radio yesterday. I simply had to pay a small fee to get it repaired and then have the use of it while I am here. It helps to add pleasure to the hours. The German stations still in operating condition are taken over by the Allies. They continue to broadcast in German but it is no longer Nazi propaganda.

We have started a German class which meets each evening for an hour. We have hired a German prof who speaks some English. We pay 10¢ each per evening. 15 officers make up the class. I'm getting a good deal out of it. We take some grammar but it is mostly the learning of much used phrases so we can get along in any business or social dealings we have with the krauts.

This evening a German civilian who has lived both in Chicago and Detroit came in to ask if I could get a message to his relatives in America. Six of the family has been killed in the bombings here. His one remaining daughter is in America and he was anxious to get some in-laws there to be responsible for her. I was so glad to discover that not only would I be able to get the message through by way of the Red Cross, but that he could also expect an answer. You can imagine his relief as he has been unable to contact them in any way for three years.

At least half a dozen have asked me about their sons in P[O]W camps in the U.S. I have assured them that they are 100% better off than those who are civilians here.

July 12, 1945 - Berlin, Germany

We have just finished our prayer service. I asked my new assistant to prepare a talk on prayer for the occasion. Only six men were there but every one of them took part on bended knee afterwards. It was a profitable hour of fellowship. The speaker had done most of his preparation with the help of [Ole] Hallesby's book on prayer which I had given him. He really presented material for thought, even though it was rather evident that he had not clearly thought through all the ideas he presented. But the practice is good for them and I am anxious to help them all I can.

Somehow I did not get to write to you yesterday. I was mighty busy throughout the day, and did not get my mail until after my German class in the evening. It was the first batch I had gotten in a long time so it took all of two hours to plow through it. Just as I was opening the first of two letters I got from you, here comes the Division Chaplain and sat until 10:30 so it was after midnight by the time I had finished reading my mail.

Your letters are so refreshing these days. You are relieved from so much strain in that you are now living in your own place, and it is plainly reflected in your letters. I feel a bit guilty, though, in the suspicion that much of your good cheer is due to your expectancy that I am just about on my way home. I wonder how much of that feeling I am responsible for. We have all been hoping that we would soon get to go and shortly after VE Day we heard so many reports which indicated that we were slated for early shipment. Now as the whole picture unfolds, we are given one lecture after the other, explaining why we are needed here and others are needed elsewhere before we can be given shipping space. Well, there is just no use fretting about it. We will try to bear it with such good grace as God gives and try to use the waiting time to good advantage.

Tomorrow I am going on an interesting mission. I have received permission to take my jeep, two assistants and my favorite Captain to travel through the country where the Reformation was born. We are taking a half dozen cameras with us and hope to return with a real picture story if only the weather is favorable. We will be gone two days so I will have no chance to write tomorrow night. We will probably spend the night with the British as we have no troops in that area. I am hoping to get some booklets as well as talk with guides and will then probably send a write-up to Faith & Fellowship. If the weather only cooperates, it should be a lovely trip and worth a lot in the way of education.

I'm enclosing another batch of pictures. All those of shelled buildings were taken in Braunschweig, Germany. I've been there a number of times, although it is now British territory.

A Lutheran Communion Service

I have today arranged for a Lutheran Communion service on Sunday afternoon. It is the first to be held in Berlin for American troops and in all probability it will be the last one held for the Lutheran men of our Division here. So it is something of an occasion and I spent all forenoon getting publicity on it to all the units. I am the only Lutheran chaplain left in the Division. Some of the lads are going to be unhappy about my not granting them absolution as they have been accustomed to and as I will not do. But if they have spiritual perception they will sense within their souls that every honest Christian among them is absolved from all his sins by a higher Authority than a mere preacher and their souls will be satisfied. If such spiritual communion is not theirs, they should not be partaking anyhow. So I do not really feel sorry for them. We have gotten the use of the Lutheran church for the occasion.

August 1, 1945 - A Furlough in Paris, France

Now I must tell you a little of what I thought of Paris. Well, the city itself is quite magnificent. Its points of scenic interest are grand. The city founders planned it with plenty of room for parks and boulevards. I have taken a sight-seeing tour over the whole city. Comparing it with

London it seems Parisians and the French generally, are much more artistic. Their architecture, monuments, and of course, their sculpture and art, emphasize more delicacy and finesse. The British are more cold and stolid. But the grandeur of both seems to center in military leaders -- here it is Napoleon and Louis XIV.

As to the people themselves, I've never liked the French. They are affected, frivolous, demonstrative and showy. Their conversation is gushy and their clothes extreme. The women surely spend half their time in beauty parlors. Their hair styles are ridiculous. "Upsweep" I suppose they call it. Generally, they wear no hats. They can't. It is no exaggeration to say that their hair which is dyed blue, purple, green, red or any color to blend with their clothes or personality, is then piled on top of their head in ringlets as high as 12 inches. It is simply unbelievable. Those who wear hats also have them built up to that height, usually with many rows of brightly colored flowers.

Did you hear the Don Cossack Choir in its broadcast from Paris on Wednesday night? Well, would you believe it, I was in the audience. Needless to say, nothing in that category ever approaches the pleasure I derive from their concerts.

I also heard a broadcast by Jeanne Froman (singer). You may remember her as the girl who traveled with the USO a couple of years ago and cracked up in a plane. She was confined to a hospital for 15 months and had 16 operations. She'll always be a cripple.

A Meeting with German Theologians

Two days ago we had a meeting of all the Chaplains in the Division with three members on the faculty of the University of Berlin. Two of them were from the theological department and one of them read a paper on the Protestant churches under Nazism. The third was a science professor and served as interpreter. The paper was very informative and I made a motion that we get the English translation mimeographed so each of us could have a copy. It showed how step by step Hitler bound and shackled the preachers so as to control all activities and the message preached. He spoke of the revolt by a large number of pastors who then paid for their insubordination by being arrested and even killed. Afterward we had a discussion on many pertinent questions. I had to have my say and haven't learned much tact yet, so I threw a bombshell into the meeting. I wanted to know how it could be that a nation which has in almost every home we have entered, crucifixes, holy pictures, prayer and hymn books besides a lot of other religious literature, and churches in abundance and such a great supply of preachers, could ever swallow such a satanic philosophy as Hitler's. I asked for the answer from a Christian and spiritual point of view. Instead, the science professor gave us the old time-honored excuse which Hitler has been feeding these Germans for over a decade. The reason was the unfair treaty of Versailles and the economic blockade by the Allies. That fired my dander and I arose to say that speaking as an individual and without representing the Chaplains, America or even the Lutheran church of which I am a pastor, that when appeals came to my church in America after the war to rebuild Protestantism in Germany, such a statement of causes would receive a mighty cold reception. I said I had hoped to hear Protestantism confess in sincere humility that the fall of Germany was not due to political or economic causes, but to the fact that modernism and Biblical criticism in seminaries and pulpits had taken the place of evangelical Christianity and had thus robbed both pulpit and pew of spiritual vision to see the danger and spiritual power to fight it. The interpreter translated and the reader of the paper said, "Thank you," and it was evident as the darky preacher said, "An uncommon coolness came over the meetin'." So even destruction, destitution, hunger and poverty have not brought a stiff-necked people to repentance -- only excuses.

August 10, 1945 - Frankfort, Germany

While we are awaiting each moment the official confirmation of the surrender of the Japs, I must write a letter. Isn't it the grandest news ever? Naturally and quite selfishly, my mind has been mostly on [younger son] Kenneth and how wonderful that he will not need to see more combat. It does not mean that he will get home for a long time, but at any rate, the hardships of combat, the prospect of maiming, injury or torturous imprisonment are over. Praise God!

Wonder what finally broke their spirit? Probably the combination of Russia's declaration of war and the atomic bomb. Certainly it is the only course that could save them from complete annihilation. Can you imagine anything like this bomb? It just has my head swimming. And to think that Germany would soon have been ready to use a similar bomb herself. I do pray that the surrender may be a true report. One cannot but feel heartsick at the thought of such death and destruction in one awful blow. I am glad that the cities have been warned. If people then choose to stay, it is largely their own responsibility. Yet, one must realize that for thousands it is humanly impossible for them to get away. There is neither transportation nor food.

In face of such devilish weapons of war, one feels that every effort must be made to postpone as long as possible, if not to avoid, another war. The human race cannot survive such destruction.

Frankfort-on-Main

As you see by this letter, I'm now in Frankfort which is some 350 miles southwest from Berlin. The whole Division made the move in three days. We camped in fields and lived on K-Rations. Quite a number of our vehicles fell out of the column with motor trouble, etc. I actually had 5 flats. When we were unable to get tire repair material, I finally had to unhook my trailer, set it up on blocks in a farmyard, take off the tires and use them on my jeep. Most of my stuff is in the trailer and it better be there when I come back for it or a certain German is going to have some questions to answer.

I got a grand break today. Since most of my stuff is in the trailer and I cannot get it before Sunday, I had to come here to see the Chaplain about the loan of some songbooks. Once in town, I was allowed to stay over-night. This wrecked city has become the U.S. Army Headquarters in Germany since VE-Day. Generals are as common here as Sergeants among combat troops. Naturally, they must have the best. The finest hotels are reserved for Officers. I'm staying at the Kaiserhof Park Hotel. Here I have a room all to myself with eiderdown covered bed, carpeted floor, divan, hot and cold water, reading lamp, dresser and wardrobe. I'm living here like a king for a day.

"Chappie, get your stuff packed, you're on your way!" was the first melodic news to reach my ears when I got back from my trip to Berlin. Of course, you cannot take an announcement like that after three years with just a grunt or even with any degree of credence. So I asked for particulars and would they please come down to earth and talk sense. Well, briefly, the story is this. Instead of waiting for two weeks to call the next batch, they are calling them this weekend and my name is on the list. Can you believe it? Together with one more Chaplain and about 2,000 of our men, I'm being transferred to the 5th Armored Division which moves out into France somewhere the first days of September and is scheduled to be alerted for a sailing date about September 15th.

Do not ask me if I'm sleeping well these nights. I don't know whether I'm in the air or on the earth. I'm having three services on Sunday, one for each of my three artillery Battalions. My principal message will be on the text: "That in all things He might have the preeminence." May it glorify the matchless Christ to whom we all, and especially I, owe such lifelong gratitude and devotion for His wondrous watchcare, patience and power through all these long months.

Still in Germany

I received a warm and cordial welcome into the Fifth Armored Division, and was assigned a home in the same house as the Artillery Commander. I rather would like to have stayed, but they may be quite as congenial in the other group. Hartfield, my assistant, took me and all my luggage down here. After we had given him a good meal and unloaded all my junk, we said good-bye.

He really surprised me. He is an unemotional man, but when we shook hands he started making a speech which he had obviously prepared for the occasion. "Chaplain, I have been dreading this moment. I've never lived and worked with a man I have admired so much, and I hate to leave you." He got no further when the tears started to roll down his cheeks, and he threw his arms around me. Then he hurried into the jeep and drove off. I had a chance to tell him how much his fellowship and cooperation had meant to me also. He's a good lad and I really love him.

Camp Atlanta, Near Rheims, France

I was permitted to travel by myself instead of in convoy so I paid a last visit to my old outfit. I picked up the mail for our boys and also my ribbon for the Presidential Citation which we had just received. Kind of pretty. I stayed one night with the outfit and another in a swell hotel in Frankfort where I had a grand bed and excellent food. Can you imagine, in the hotel lobby were two nurses who had been on the same boat as I when we went to Africa 2 years ago. I did not remember them but they recognized me and said they had never forgotten the sermon I preached on Good Friday on board the ship. They were headed for Marseilles where they were to ship for home.

We had a Chaplain's meeting this morning. There appears to be about ten Chaplains in this bunch on their way -- just two of us came from the 2nd [Armored Division]. We arranged services for the camp for this Sunday. Two of us will share each service, making five Protestant services for the camp which is adequate. Most of the Chaplains wanted no Sunday evening service, but I said I did. I have plenty of time, why shouldn't I if the men wanted to come? And they will. There are only two movie places and no town to go to. There are no lights in our tents and as it is dark early, the evenings get pretty long. I went to bed at 9:00 p.m. last night. The officers had gotten their liquor yesterday and their conversation was, as a consequence, hardly to my taste.

August 14, 1945 - Langendeibach , Germany

This is Sunday morning. Can you imagine me having time to write letters? Well, it happens that I have only one service this morning and another this afternoon. This combined with the fact that I have been having my sermon in mind all week gives me some time to talk to you this morning.

The sermon is based on John 1:14-15: "And the Word became flesh and dwelt among us and we beheld his glory, full of grace and truth." So we came to know God only when His Son came among us. Now the truth that is especially practical to my men today after a week in the rain and mud, is based on the first half of this Scripture. Weymouth translates it: "And the Word became flesh and lived awhile in our midst." But Goodspeed [translates it]: "The Word became flesh and pitched his tent among us." That's the word for us today. It is a truth: 1) Of Sublime Condescension. To think that the Lord of Heaven laid aside His "rank" and glory, that He forsook His wealth and "for our sakes became poor," that though infinitely wise, He patiently bore with our ignorance and stupidity and though spotlessly pure, He shared our sin and degradation. What a Wonderful Saviour! 2) It is also a truth of Blessed Companionship. Every soldier notices how much more companionable and accessible an officer is when out in the field than when hc is in garrison. The Old Testament God could be reached through the priest and settle man's accounts once a year. But Jesus' name also means Emmanuel -- God with us. Now He can be reached "in any time of need." 3) The truth is also one of Hopeful Anticipation. Even the army does not put us up in tents for a permanent residence. We live together there for just a little while to move into better "quarters." "I go to prepare a place for you -- that where I am there ye may be also." "I'm going higher, yes, higher some day, I'm going higher some day."

So much for the sermon. We now have a roof over our heads once more. We have moved into a little town about 15 miles from Frankfort. It is an old place and most of the house is smelly and the furniture poor. As usual, the farmers live right in the village and all the barnyard smells permeate the whole town. However, I feel that men are somewhat easier to control in a small place like this. I am sure that after a bit, arrangements will be made whereby they can get into Frankfort for movies and parties, and that is by far the best arrangement. Then we haul them into town in trucks and they come home the same way. We know where they are at all times.

I have gotten churches for both of my services today. After we get more settled, I will probably have a service in each of the several small towns where our troops are. For today, I have asked them to come to two central churches.

This morning I received your two packages containing sardines and chicken soup, Thanks. They're always welcome. Hope I may get some coffee one of these days. Of course, it may be very difficult for you to get it. I know nothing about your rationing, so please do not deprive yourself of what you need.

August 20, 1945 - Frankfort, Germany

In the blustery downpour of this eternal rain, the first batch of post-war GI's and Officers left the area this morning to start their trek homeward. The weather did nothing whatsoever to dampen their spirits, however. From this Battalion with its thirty officers, only one man went. He is a Professor from Purdue and as fine a man as they come. He has been as faithful in his attendance at church services as anyone could ask.

Had a talk with the Division Chaplain last night. Most important in our conversation was the fact that he told me that the two Chaplains who had said they wanted to stay in the army, are going home today. They are the highest point men we have -- 128 and 132. Now the next Chaplain is 119 and then I come with 117. So even including the "Yes" men [those wanting to stay in the Army], I'm well up toward the top again. If I do not make it in this next batch in two weeks, it will certainly not be more than a month. That you can count on.

Then the Division Chaplain offered me a job as Regimental Chaplain. It would finally mean a promotion and I could retire as a Major. But then to be decent about it, I would have to choose to stay in for a while. That I cannot see myself doing. There would be no greater service that I could render the men by such a change, and there would be nothing in it financially either, for such a short time. So I'm staying where I am until I hear the boat whistle.

Another matter came up yesterday that interested me far more. I heard of the possibility of flying to Palestine on a seven-day leave. Can you imagine anything grander for one's own Christian life and ministry than to have visited all those sacred places. It would be the fulfillment of a dream which I had never dared to hope would be realized. It is all too uncertain yet for me to give you any details, but I feel sure you will want me to make the trip if it is at all possible. In peacetime such a trip would cost me at least $2000. Now it would not cost $50. I would be traveling with a group of Chaplains from the Mediterranean and would go by way of Rome and Cairo, Egypt. Will you hope with me that it can be made possible?

This morning I must be off on a trip to Berlin. I have a serious soldier's case to investigate and also am to have an interview with the Theological Professor from the Berlin U. I may be gone three days and do not know what chance I will have to write, but will get off letters just as often as I can.

September 17, 1945 - LaHavre, France

Seems kind of silly to be writing to you as it is entirely possible that I will be there to remove the letter from the mailbox when it arrives.

The rumors of our sailing date are still good. The Port Authorities were notified this noon that the Division is now ready to load. Now it's up to them to assign us ships as they come in. We are hearing now that we will certainly be out of here this week.

In the meantime I'm using my time the best I can. Sunday I had two grand services. In the morning we crowded 300 men into the chapel and quite a number were turned away. In the evening I again had the only service in camp, and fully 150 men turned out. I told them that if they cared to come out, I'd have a service for them every evening. They said, "Sure," so tonight (Monday) I've just had a service for over 200 men. Best of all, two of them accepted Christ.

We had real inspiring singing and a swell testimony service. One said it was the first chance he had been given for a public testimony in three years in the army. Another lad was a Puerto Rican who was going to return to his home island as a witness. A third was a son of Rinden's at Joice, Iowa. It was a blessed evening I can tell you. I expect to have services every day on board ship, too.

September 19, 1945 - Still in France

Today is the day we were originally scheduled to load on a ship for home. Instead, there hasn't been a good rumor until tonight, when I'm told we'll be loading on Monday.

Needless to say, almost everyone is simply bored to death. They have absolutely nothing to do. I am one of the fortunate ones. My meeting keeps me busy every evening and gives me a chance to burn up my energy and really go to bed tired. During the day I must study and make arrangements for organists and special singing. So I have my hands full and the time passes both pleasantly and swiftly.

The meetings have been swell. The attendance has increased from about 175 on Sunday night to all of 250 this evening. Their interest is thrilling. Tonight there were five Chaplains at the service. Several sincerely regret they did not have services in their area and two have frankly admitted that it was simply because they gave in to the temptation to loaf. God pity us with such opportunities knocking at our doors. Every evening men have surrendered to Christ. Tonight there were 10 or 11. I had gotten a Negro quartet to sing two songs. There is just nothing in the world that compares with preaching the gospel of Christ to the salvation of sinners! I never cease to marvel that God is able to bless such an unworthy instrument.

September 20, 1945 - Still at Camp 20 Grand, La Havre, France

It certainly looks as though Uncle Sam is going to have to pay me another full month of overseas pay. We're still waiting for ships but the rumor prevails they'll get us out of here the first of next week.

I had an interesting visit yesterday. In the morning a Sergeant Soholt, son of the banker in Mayville, came to see me. He has a desk job with the Division which is operating this camp and had seen my name on the shipping list. He has been converted since coming into the army and we had a blessed visit ending with a season on our knees at the altar of our little chapel.

And we're still having grand times at our services. Last night 23 men dedicated their lives to Christian service. Many men declare it's the greatest experience they've had in the army -- this week of meetings. The attendance holds at about 250 each night.

I had a grand experience with one fellow last night. He told me after the service that he had asked for prayer 14 months ago in England, but he had no joy and could not leave the tent without finding it. So I sat down with him to explain that joy is not the source of a Christian experience, but that it is the fruit of the Spirit. The fruit follows being born of the Spirit which takes place when we meet God's conditions and then take Him at His Word in simple faith. We settled on 1 John 1:9* and showed him there what God required and what God then promised -- forgiveness and cleansing. I explained this and he admitted he had never accepted God's truth as here revealed. When asked if he would do so now, he determinedly said he would. We bowed our knees and I prayed. I asked him to pray. When he could not, I asked him to repeat a prayer after me. This he did until he said, "And now I thank Thee that thou dost accept me as thy child." Then his voice broke and he flung his arms around my neck and as the tears of joy flowed down his cheeks, he repeated over and over, "Thank you, Jesus. Thank you, Jesus." I didn't need to ask if he'd found Christ. I didn't need to ask if he'd found the joy he sought. Another soul went to his tent set free and rejoicing.

So while I yearn to get on that boat and start for home, God is giving us showers of blessing here, as rich as I've had since the blessed campaign we had in England. It is going to mean that many of these men will return to their homes in a week or two to tackle their civilian problems and take their place in family and community as new creatures. The far-reaching effect can hardly be imagined.

One of our Chaplains, a very gifted Major, openly testified in the meeting last night that the message on Monday evening led to a rededication of his life to proclaiming the gospel of salvation. He said he had grown so cold, careless and lazy, that he has wasted so many golden opportunities. I needed this time of spiritual, refreshing myself, and praise God for it.

*["If we confess our sins, he is faithful and just to forgive us our sins, and to cleanse us from all unrighteousness."]

September 23, 1945 - La Havre, France

This will be a new experience: writing a letter at 7:30 Sunday morning. But I have some time now because the area Chaplain decided that after I had built up the attendance to a full chapel every night, while he was sitting at the movie, that it would look good on his monthly report to show that he had a capacity crowd this morning. Accordingly, he informed me that he would take the service this morning. I will visit his service at 11:00 a.m. and another at 10:00 a.m. [sic], but I will not preach this morning. I have a service, however, at 7:00 p.m.

Little did we think last Sunday that we would still be in Europe today. Each day we've been expecting to hear of the arrival of our ships, but to date the harbor is quiet. I understand the West Point did arrive, but they loaded on it some remnants of other Divisions which had been laying around here for some time and some small groups which belonged to no Division.

In the meantime rumors have been flying about concerning certain of our high rank officers who will lose their jobs when they get home and so are delaying our sailing date as long as possible. Also, there is bitterness and much complaint about army inefficiency.

It hasn't gotten me down at all until yesterday. It may be that the fact that I am coming down with a peach of a cold had something to do with the landslide of my morale. But we have been on the way for more than a month and certainly have not made much progress. In the meantime, our fall schedule which depends on my return is being knocked into a cocked hat. But God knows I'm here and He knows all of us are. Romans 8:28* must cover this situation, too. I know it has meant the salvation of souls and the restoration of backsliders. Though flesh and blood cries out for release from this place, in my heart I know the time has not been wasted.

In this situation, you can well imagine that these 12,000 men get to be quite a problem. No explanation makes sense to them. Cooped up as they are in camp, with nothing to do, they grow bitter and feel like convicts. To let them off to towns on pass in their mental condition is risky because they'll only get into trouble. As Chaplain I feel that our best answer is the service every evening. There they blow off steam in enthusiastic singing and the fellowship and message warms the heart. I understand the Division is today going to start an extensive league of ball games to try to keep scores of them occupied. We'll certainly need to pool all of our resources and ingenuity to keep Mr. Gloom at bay. The army is no place for a civilian soldier when the fighting is over. I'm glad I did not apply for a job in regular army.

*["And we know that all things work together for good to them that love God, to them who are the called according to his purpose."]

HOME AT LAST!

The U.S. Army Transport Alexander finally docked at La Havre and we were loaded on board. We could not have had a better trip. We were six Chaplains on board and we held two services every day in addition to scores of conferences with the men. The officers had comfortable accommodations, but the enlisted men as usual were crowded below deck. The food was the best we had ever had in the army.

After six pleasant days we were on deck before daylight to catch the first glimpse of the U.S.A. Through the golden glow of the sunrise, we gradually made out the shore line and within an hour we were sailing into the narrows of New York harbor. There on the embankment were inscribed in large letters and painted snow-white: "Welcome Home! Well Done!" To us that greeting was as real as if it were spoken by the united voice of America.

After the seemingly endless red tape of checking our records, final exams and going over our equipment, we were given a real welcome; assured that we would presently have a steak dinner with ice cream and real milk, and then would have a few minutes to ourselves. Just one question was on everyone's lips, "Where can I find a telephone and call my folks?" We found that an excellent telephone service had been installed at the camp. Inside of a matter of minutes I heard a voice over the wire of which I had only dreamed for almost three years. Within two days we had a chance to be together for a few hours and together on bended knee we sought to express in words our gratitude to our Lord who had so wondrously protected us through all these weary months of separation.

EPILOGUE

As I now view in retrospect these three and one-half years in uniform, several facts stand out crystal clear. First, I have had a chance to test the faithfulness of God and His promises through imminent death, hardships and terrific testings. I have the confidence that I was given the opportunity to enjoy one of the richest times of spiritual fruitfulness that has been mine in more than twenty years in the ministry. I have seen that a consecrated and separated Christian life lived humbly day by day, wins the respect and confidence of the most ungodly. I have a profound admiration for the way in which the Lutheran Church kept in touch with their members and Chaplains. I feel very much indebted to the National Lutheran Council and especially to the Lutheran Service Commission and its capable and conscientious director, Dr. N. N. Ylvisaker, who gave us invaluable aid and excellent supplies for our work. I am grateful to my own Synod and my congregation for giving me permission to enter the service.

I praise God for the staunch courage and steadfastness of my wife during these trying years and wish to register also my indebtedness to the many Christians throughout the land who upheld me in prayer. I trust that I may now bring to my work in my congregation a deeper sympathy, a warmer friendliness, a stauncher faith and a more whole-hearted consecration since God has seen fit to spare my life for further service.

Appendix A: In Memorium

Faith and Fellowship newsletter, August 1982

Rev. Clarence Walstad, 78, Fulton, Texas, died unexpectedly on Tuesday morning, July 13. Funeral services were conducted at Ebenezer Lutheran Brethren Church, Minneapolis, July 16, where he was a member. Lutheran Brethren President Everald Strom and former Lutheran Brethren President Dan Erickson officiated at the services.

Walstad was born in Mohall, North Dakota, October 29, 1903, and was raised in the foster home of Mr. & Mrs. C. C. Habberstad. He was married to Ruth Bridston in 1923.

Rev. Walstad served as a Lutheran Brethren pastor and a chaplain in the United States Armed Services during World War II. He served as the first full-time president of the Church of the Lutheran Brethren and was an able evangelist and preacher of the Gospel.

He is survived by his wife, Ruth; two sons, Kenneth and Robert; a daughter, Marilyn Kranz; nine grandchildren and three great-grandchildren; a foster brother, Chester Habberstad, and a foster sister, Hazel Holstrom.

The next issue will carry a tribute from Lutheran Brethren President Everald Strom.

Appendix B: A Tribute to Clarence Walstad

By Everald H. Strom

It was morning – shortly after breakfast – that Clarence E, Walstad quietly left this world [July 13, 1982] to be with the Lord. He was 78 years old at the time of his passing. Thus ended a life that left a significant imprint upon the Church of the Lutheran Brethren in this generation.

He was a dynamic individual with a captivating personality and was gifted as a leader. People were drawn to him as a person and enjoyed being part of his fellowship circle. He was a master as a public speaker and as such exercised great influence both in and out of the pulpit. Possessed of limitless energy, he gave himself to the tasks at hand with real vigor and determination. He loved the church of the Lutheran Brethren and was most happy when he could be involved in its ministry.

At an early age he came to assurance of salvation. He loved his Lord and had a deep appreciation for the atonement of Christ. Psalm 130 was one of his favorites, and it gave testimony to the fact that the anchor of His soul held tightly to the grace and mercy of God. This is the refuge of all those whose citizenship is in heaven.

Clarence Walstad served the Church of the Lutheran Brethren as a pastor and as an able evangelist. Over the years, many lives came to repentance and faith through his gift of evangelism. When the office of synodical president became a full time position, he was elected to that position and served the synod several years in that capacity. He also served on several of the synodical boards and in particular spent many years as a member of the Board of Trustees where he served with distinction. As an elder in Ebenezer Lutheran Church of Minneapolis, Minnesota, it was his privilege to minister effectively to the spiritual needs of the congregation for a period of several years.

During World War II he felt called to enter military service and was attached to the 2nd Armored Division in Europe. One of the soldiers attached to that unit spoke of it as "an awesome sight to see that big man [6'4"] crawling from foxhole to foxhole with a message of comfort and encouragement from the Lord to frightened and anxious soldiers during the heat of battle."

The life of Clarence Walstad is now completed, but it is appropriate for us as a Church of the Lutheran Brethren to thank God for his ministry and for the imprint which he left upon the Church of Jesus

Christ. He departed this world as a pilgrim whose entrance into the presence of Christ was based solely on the redemption made possible at Calvary. We thank God for this testimony and the encouragement it gives to other pilgrims as they make their way to God's promised land.

Appendix C: Clergy Record, Albin Funeral Chapel

Albin Funeral Chapel
Ralph Albinson, Director
Paul Albinson, Founder
2200 Nicollet Avenue
Minneapolis, Minnesota 55404

Clarence E. Walstad was born in Mohall, North Dakota, on October 29, 1903. Before he was 4 years old his mother died and it became necessary for him to be raised by foster parents – CC. Habberstad of Underwood, Minnesota.

When he was 16 he left the foster home and sought to make his own way. On November2, 1923, he and Ruth Bridston were married.

He attended the University of California at Berkley for a while, but then, after determining that he wanted to enter Christian work, he transferred to the Denver Bible Institute. From there he went into Home Mission work for the Lutheran Brethren Church of America and attended the Lutheran Brethren Seminary. He accepted a call to the Norwegian Free Church in Brooklyn, New York, to serve as youth worker and Assistant Pastor.

His service there was interrupted after several years by a call to be Pastor of the Ebenezer Lutheran Brethren Church in Minneapolis. Some time later, the Brooklyn Church called Rev. Walstad to return as their Pastor. This he did.

It was while he was there that the United States entered World War II. Shortly thereafter, Rev. Walstad decided to follow the young men overseas and minister to their spiritual needs there. He applied for the Chaplaincy Corps and was accepted. On April 14, 1943, Lt. Clarence Walstad was on a troop ship overseas. For the next two and a half years he served his God, his country and his men.

Fortunately the day did come when the Walstad family was again united. During his service career Mr. Walstad won 5 campaign ribbons for service. He was awarded a Bronze Star with special citation and also a Presidential Citation [and] the Belgian Unit Citation. After serving in the Army Reserves, he was honorably discharged on April 1, 1953 and returned to serve the church in Brooklyn.

In 1951 he was elected President of the Lutheran Brethren Synod. In 1956 he entered the field of insurance [Mutual Security Life

Insurance Company]. Clarence was as successful in business as he had been in other endeavors. He received many awards for excellence of service.

He retired from his Minneapolis business in 1976. He was told by his doctor to seek a milder climate so he moved to Rockport, Texas. Despite poor health, he taught a Men's Bible Class each Sunday at First Baptist Church of Rockport until his death on July 13, 1982. Clarence lived to the age of 78 yrs., 8 months & 14 days.

He is survived by:

His wife, Ruth of Rockport, Texas

Two sons, Kenneth of Minneapolis, Minn. & Robert of Dallas, Texas

One daughter, Marilyn Kranz of Live Oak, Florida.

9 grandchildren &

3 great-grandchildren

The interment will follow this service in Oak Hill Cemetery.

Thank You.

Made in the USA
Columbia, SC
29 November 2020